25 Walks in Nort

This book has been published to mark the 25th /
Ramblers. We offer a wide ranging all year prc
evening walks. Check our website: www

The 25 walks are based on a book published in 1987 by three of our members. The walks have been reassessed, routes improved and new walks added. We have tried to cater for all tastes and for varying levels of fitness. A general knowledge of map and compass will make the walks more interesting and this is recommended particularly on the hills.

The Ordnance Survey Maps for North Ayrshire are:
Landranger 63, 69 and 70 Explorer 333 and 341

Grid References are included in almost all the walk descriptions – these are bracketed in red. Distances are given in miles and total height climbed (THC) in metres are included where appropriate. Walk times have not been included but a general rule of thumb is 2 miles per hour. This allows for photos and refreshment stops.

Cunninghame Ramblers are grateful for financial assistance from North Ayrshire Council, without whose help the book would have remained a pipedream. Nicolson Maps have been a great support on mapping, layout, editing & publishing.

Although every effort has been made to ensure accuracy in route description and mapping, Cunninghame Ramblers cannot accept responsibility for any accident or injury by walkers on these walks. Common sense, knowledge of the Scottish Outdoor Access Code, basic road safety and awareness of your own level of fitness will go a long way to ensure your safe enjoyment of these walks.

Our members have devoted many hours in preparing and publishing this book and their reward will be seeing and hearing of those who have used the book as an aid in enjoying the nature, history and magnificent scenery of North Ayrshire.

Happy rambling!

Mapping © Nicolson Maps PU398098 © Crown copyright reserved
Based on the Ordnance Survey map with the permission of Her Majesty's Stationery Office. Unauthorised reproduction by any means infringes copyright.
The grid on this map is the National Grid taken from the Ordnance Survey map with the permission of The Controller of Her Majesty's Stationery Office.

Scottish Outdoor Access Code

Scotland's outdoors is the home of diverse wildlife, trees, flowers and plants and is enjoyed by the many people who live there and visit it, as well as where land managers make a living. Please exercise your access rights responsibly by following the key principles of the Scottish Outdoor Access Code:

1. Take responsibility for your own actions. The outdoors cannot be made risk-free for people exercising access rights

2. Respect the interests of other people. Be considerate, respect privacy and livelihoods, and the needs of those enjoying the outdoors. When close to a house or garden, keep a sensible distance from the house, use a path or track if there is one, and take extra care at night.

3. Care for your environment. Look after the places you visit and enjoy. Care for wildlife and historic sites Do not disturb wildlife, leave the environment as you find it. Follow a path or track wherever there is one.

4. Help land managers and others to work safely and effectively. Do not hinder land management operations and follow advice from land managers. Respect requests for reasonable limitations on when and where you can go.

5. Keep your dog under proper control. Do not take it through fields of calves and lambs and dispose of dog dirt.

6. Take extra care if you are organising an event or running a business. Ask the land owner's advice.

To find out more about your own responsibilities, or to download a copy of the full Scottish Outdoor Access Code, please visit:

www.outdooraccess-scotland.com

To order your own copy of the code, please phone: 01738 458545 or email pubs@snh.gov.uk

Index to Walks

Walk		Area	Grade
1	Irvine Historical	Irvine	C
2	Irvine to Tarryholme Ponds	Irvine	C
3	Bowertrapping Wood	Dalry	C+
4	Cuff Hill	Beith	B
5	Irvine to Dreghorn	Irvine	C+
6	Irvine Harbour & Beachpark	Irvine	C
7	Dreghorn to Eglinton Park	Dreghorn	B
8	Stanecastle to Girdle Toll	Irvine	C
9	Seamill & West Kilbride	West Kilbride	C
10	A Dauner round Dalry	Dalry	C+
11	Goldenberry Hill	West Kilbride	B
12	North Hill	Ardrossan	B+
13	Kaim Hill	Fairlie	B+
14	Three Towns Walk	Saltcoats, Stevenston & Ardrossan	C+
15	Douglas Park	Largs	B+
16	Rowantree Hill	Largs	B+
17	Blaeloch	Fairlie	B+
18	Ladyford to Cockston	Kilbirnie	B
19	Irish Law	Largs	B+
20	Cauldron Hill Linear	West Kilbride – Fairlie	B
21	Glaid Stone	Greater Cumbrae	C
22	Glenashdale Falls	Arran	C+
23	Bridges and Burns	Arran	C+
24	Cock of Arran	Arran	B
25	Clauchland Hills	Arran	B

Key to Walks

C	Easy walking.
C+	Easy walking but might involve a slight ascent.
B	Longer than a 'C', over 8 miles and could involve some climbing
B+	Rough ground and will involve climbing

Walk 1: Irvine Historical

Grade: C   Distance: 2.5 miles   Paths & pavements

1 Park in the car park near Irvine Cross. Turn right out of the car park and do down Puddleford Lane known locally as Puddlie Doodlie steps to the River Irvine which originally led to the Puddle Ford, the scene of a battle between Wallace's troops and the English, hence the Puddly Deidle, the deadly fight. Next turn left along the riverside path and at the end of the path is St Inan's Well, now dried up. St Inan was the Patron Saint of Irvine.

2 Go up the steps past Glebe Primary school and onto the open ground observe the white building, the former Town Powder House built in 1642. Here gunpowder had to be stored beyond the town walls for safety. Retrace your steps past the well and follow path under shopping mall to reach the Low Green. The 1994 monument to the Trades Guild is an interesting point. Carry on heading out of town to reach the statue of Robert Burns.

3 The bronze statue of Robert Burns (1759 – 1796) was erected in 1896, 100 years after his death. Head back along the path till you reach the swings and turn left into Castle Street. The statue here is of David Boyle (1772 -1853), former Lord Justice General of Scotland. From here turn right into Seagate.

4 Seagate Castle dates back to 1565 and was visited by Mary Queen of Scots, hence the annual August Marymass Festival organised by the Trades Guild. At the end of Seagate, turn right into High Street and look on the wall of no 167 High Street for a plaque which commemorates the Irvine-born writer, John Galt (1779 – 1839), whose acclaimed books include The Annals of the Parish and the biography The Life of Byron.

5 Walk on through the Cross observing the Town House on your left. Built in 1860, it is now the District Court and scene of the crowning of the Marymass Queen.

6 Passing the War Memorial, walk on along Townhead and turn right into the cobbled Glasgow Vennel. The Heckling Shop (a shop used to process flax) where Burns lived and worked for a short time is at no. 10.

7 Go back across the main road into Kirk Vennel and visit Irvine Parish Church built in 1774. Its graveyard contains many interesting headstones. Exit into Kirkgate and retrace your steps to the start of the walk.

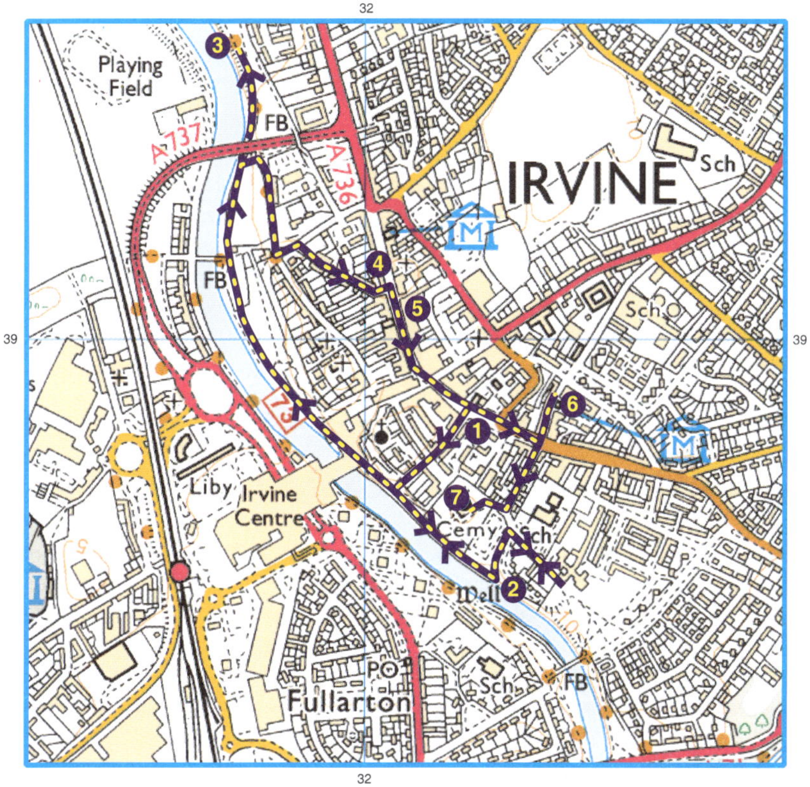

Seagate Castle

Powder House

Walk 2: Irvine to Tarryholme Ponds

Grade: C   Distance 4 - 4.5 miles   Paths & pavements

The walk starts at the Town House at Irvine Cross. (NS322388) There are various car parks in Irvine adjacent to the starting point of the walk.

1 Cross the road and walk up Kirkgate. At the end of this street you will be facing a lane, Puddleford (known locally as the Puddly Doodly). Go down the steps to the River Irvine. Turn left to walk along the lower path running parallel to the river. Proceed along this path walking between the river and the old cemetery wall. Keep on the path till it veers to the left. This is St Innans Well – St Innan being the patron saint of Irvine. (NS323385)

2 Go up the steps facing you, turn right and walk past Glebe Primary School. After a few yards you pass Red Cross House and exit on to the Golfields. On the right you will see an interesting, octagonal building, the Town Powder House. Keep straight on the path till you come to a grey bridge. Ignore the bridge and go straight on up the path through the trees. You will come to a Bailey Bridge carrying the main road. Go down the steps then up to exit into Tarryholme Park. (NS325381)

3 Follow the riverside path till it meets the River Annick. When you reach a black bridge cross it keeping to the path till you reach Tarryholme Estate. Turn right and walk along the pavement. At the last house take the path ahead of you and soon you will reach the first pond. Take the first right and walk round the pond. (NS329376)

4 Just before completing the pond circuit, turn right and cross the road. Go round the second pond taking time to admire the wildlife. At the end of second pond circuit leave the path and turn right. At the main road, turn right at the roundabout and walk along the pavement. After a short distance you will reach some houses. Cross the road and take the path alongside these houses until you arrive at a blue bridge. (NS328381)

5 Cross it and turn left and left again, bringing you back to the River Annick path. Keep walking till you reach the main Irvine – Dreghorn Road (NS330385)

6 Cross the road at the lights and take the path signposted Kilmarnock circling the hotel. Watch out for stray golf balls! As you go round the hotel, go under a road bridge and soon you will reach a red foot bridge over the river. Cross it and you will now be on the bus route. Turn left and walk along Mill Road to the end, then turn right and make your way back to the Town Hall.

The Powder House, originally named 'Pouther' (old Scots for 'powder') House is one of the few surviving in Scotland and was thought to have been first built in 1642. James VI of Scotland had instructed that all Royal burghs should have powder magazines and the saltpetre (potassium nitrate) would have been stored in the Powder House, for the manufacturing of gunpowder. Its reconstruction was completed in 1801 and it ceased being used in 1880.

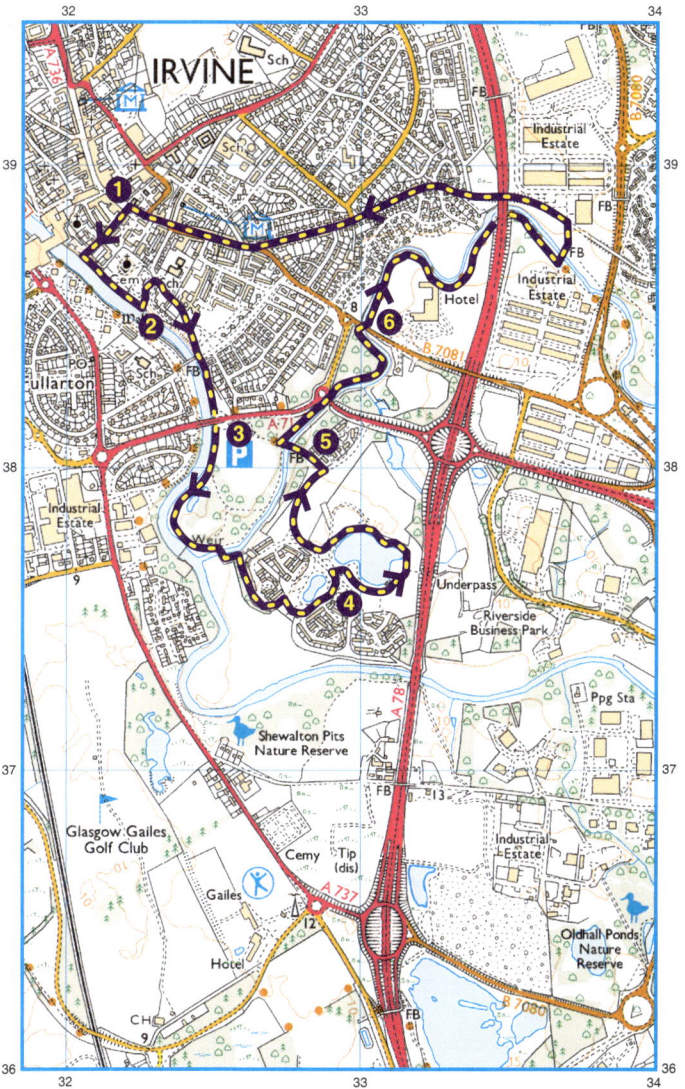

Walk 3: Bowertrapping Woods

Grade: C+   Distance 8miles, THC 215metres   Bridle paths, tracks & quiet roads

This is a pleasant walk through rolling, largely unfrequented countryside which is idyllic in any season. There is scope for optional loops and shorter walks. Wild flowers and herons abound, as well as other wildlife. The bridle paths can be muddy, and the long grass wet, depending on weather, so boots should be worn. Please abide by the instructions of Blair Estate when using estate paths and bridle paths.

Parking: Take the A737 to Dalry and turn into the minor road past Dalry Railway Station. Follow this road through the Blair housing estate and past the North Gate of the Blair Estate. At the T- junction turn left and park in the lay-by a short distance up the road, locally known as The Loanings. (NS309491)

1 The walk starts at the T- junction at the north gate of the Blair Estate. If you have come by car, retrace the road back to start. At the T-junction, you will find a track to the left, alongside the Bombo Burn, at a Walkers Welcome sign. This walk is well way-marked and easy to follow using the white arrows indicating the bridle paths and the green and orange Walkers signs. Follow the track, taking a sharp right turn at Lambridden Stud Farm and then on to Blair Pit (closed in the 1960s). Go through the gate and follow the bridle path onto a tree-covered ridge, which has good views on a clear day. Proceed along the ridge until Bowertrapping Farm comes into view. At this point the track becomes vague but it curves across the field and heads for a gate near a prominent bridle path sign. Go through the gate and take the walker's loop on the right. Shortly after the walkers sign, you can take the left fork and follow the loop (pleasant ½ hour detour) in a clockwise direction back to the bridle path sign. Continue on the bridle path past various small woods till it reaches the minor road at Pencot Farm. (NS328492)

2 Turn right on to the road and follow it until you reach a small hill on the left and a kissing gate. Go through the gate and take the loop marked Walkers Way to the trig point at the top of this hill. Again, this has excellent views on a clear day. (NS327488)

3 Follow the circular loop back to the kissing gate, then the bridle path signs past Pencot Farm, which has historic WW2 Nissen shelters. The path now swings through woodland to follow the Dusk Water then up a rise to the minor road near the cottage at Foxcover Plantation. This is the end of the way-marked section. On reaching the road, turn left and follow the road up above the Dusk Water until you meet a T-junction. (NS320478)

4 Turn left on to this minor road past several Z-bends and past the picturesque Blair Mill, now a private dwelling. Cross over the Dusk Water and take the minor road immediately to the right. Just past Stenhouse on the right, look for a fence among the hedgerow. Go through the gap at the side of the fence and follow the distinct woodland path to the gorge overlooking the Dusk Water. You are now standing on top of the cave system known as Cleeves Cove. Retrace the path back to the road and turn right. Follow the road past Auchenskeith Farm till it meets the T-junction with the road. Turn right onto the

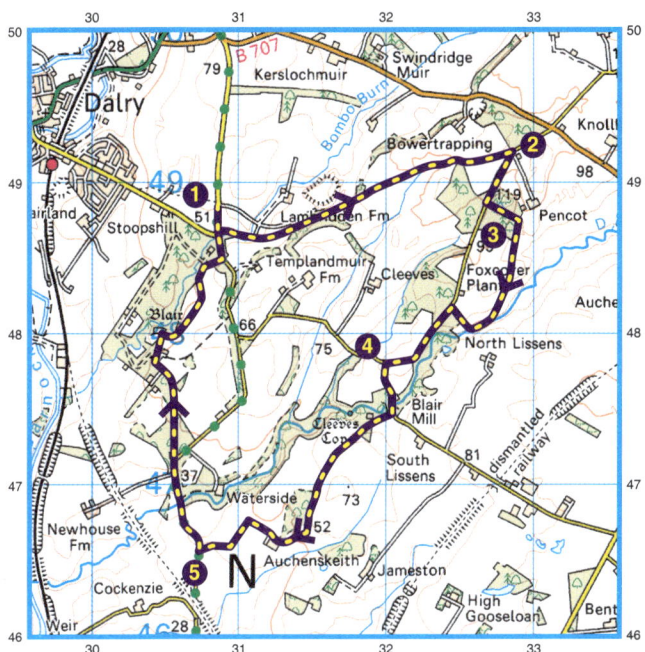

oad, taking care as it is a busy road and is part of the National Cycle Route.
NS307466)

The road falls and rises through a picturesque dip over the Dusk Water, past Newhouse arm gates to reach the South Gate of Blair Estate. The picturesque grounds of this well-maintained estate make a pleasant, short walk in their own right and are well-used by ocals. Follow the estate driveway, past the woodland and farmland, past the old stables nd past Blair House, parts of which date from the 13th century, over a couple of rnamental bridges until the North Gate is reached. Turn right onto the road, walk to the -junction, turn left and walk back to the parking place if you came by car.

Cleeves Cove ('Cove' being the Scots word for 'cave') is a limestone cave system, which, when excavated, was found to contain prehistoric animal bones, ancient man-made artifacts and charcoal deposits. In the 17th Century, The Covenanters took efuge in the caves from their persecution by Charles II and by Victorian times, Cleeves Cove was recognised as one of Ayrshire's greatest natural phenomena. More recently, Cleeves Cove has been a field trip destination for geographers and geologists. Entry to he caves is hazardous and difficult and not recommended unless properly trained and quipped.

Walk 4 : Cuff Hill

Grade: B   Distance: 7 miles   THC 286 metres   Pavements, quiet roads & open ground.

Recommended time: September – April to avoid long grass and summer growth

The walk starts at Beith Cross. (NS349539) Bellman's Close and Dickson Court car parks are near Beith Town centre and are well signposted.

1 The Auld Kirk at Beith Cross, for long a ruin, has connections with the Rev John Wotherspoon, the only clergyman to sign the American Declaration of Independence. From the cross go NW through the narrow Main Street, past the memorial to Henry Faulds, a pioneer of fingerprinting. Main Street becomes Wilson Street and leads to Trinity Church. Just before the church, turn right up Threepwood Road (un-named). This soon reaches the A737 bypass. Cross this busy highway with care and follow Threepwood Road to Beith Golf Course. The road passes the Grange Estate, through farm land, taking a sharp left hand bend before ascending a steep hill. Views over Kilbirnie Hills and Lochwinnoch open up and Ben Lomond can be seen on a clear day. Past the Golf Clubhouse, the road plateaus out and descends to St Inan's Well opposite a cottage. Just after the spring is a farm track to High Bogside. (NS371554)

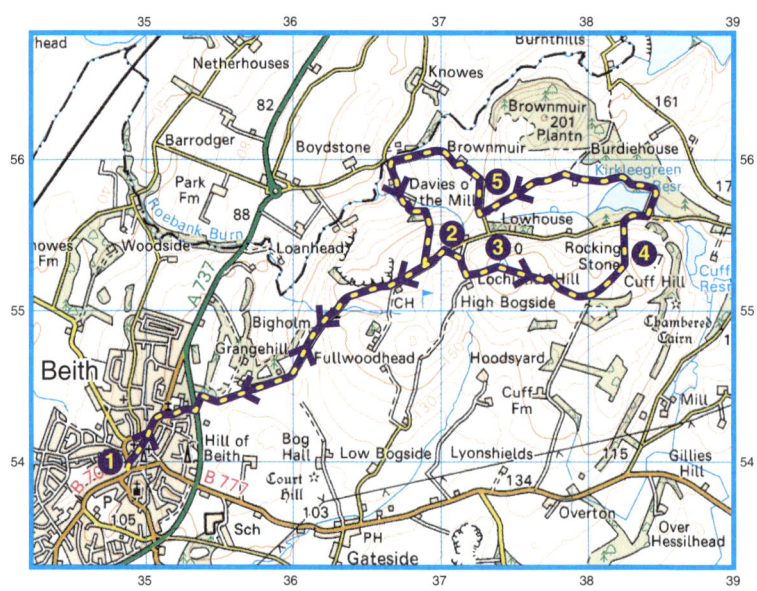

Turn along the track and immediately go through a gate on the left, just below a footpath which strikes up the side of Lochlands Hill. Go right up the footpath past a rock niche known as St Inan's Chair. Follow the path till it peters out and head for the mast. Follow the dyke running at right angles to the mast to the trig point at the top, easily spotted on the other side of the dyke. (NS374553)

Follow the dyke down till you come to a dyke with a wooden barrier. Cross here, turn right to join a track following the original dyke, then turn left along a rough but clear track. Follow this track going through a gate to the left of some trees. In summer, these fields contain cattle so exercise caution. Without losing height, follow this track till it reaches another gate. Go through this gate and then a second gate and look for a track going north, glimpsing the chambered cairn and Cuffhill Reservoir below. The woodland fringes the slopes of Cuff Hill. An attractive lochan occupies the hilltop area. After passing the lochan, veer left and head for a group of trees which contain the Rocking Stone, a large erratic rock left behind when the ice retreated during the last Ice Age. It no longer rocks, however. (NS382554)

From the stone head downhill aiming for a gate onto Threepwood Road. Turn right and follow the road round a hairpin bend to the dam at Kirkleegreen Reservoir, just beside the road. Walk halfway across the dam and over a small bridge. Follow a narrow track alongside the reservoir. This is very overgrown in summer. Take care crossing the burn and continue as the path winds between the fence and the bracken-covered hillside. When the bracken stops, strike up over the hillside till you reach the ruins of Rakerfield. This was probably a bleach field. Turn left following the rough track behind the cottages leading to the main track. Turn left and continue until a gate leading to a minor road is reached. (NS372556)

Turn right onto this road, following it down hill past Brownmuir Farm almost as far as the bridge at Mill of Beith, by an attractive waterfall. Before the bend in the road at the bridge are two gates on the left. Pass round the upper or left hand gate, blocked by boulders, and follow a wide track going SE to Davies o' the Mill. This is a right of way, but at the time of writing, the sign and most of the way marked posts had disappeared, however, Loanhead Quarry is very obvious. After a short walk the ruin of Davies o' the Mill is reached. Early spring brings an attractive display of snowdrops. The right of way now becomes very indistinct but follows a track past the ruined outbuildings to the left. Follow the path for 200 yards to an opening in the fence. Carry straight on for another 100 yards and turn right at the marker post, then climb up through woodland until a ladder stile is reached. Go over the stile to a gorse-covered hillside and make your way as best you can up and over the hill. Keep the dyke close by on the left until another ladder stile, leading to Threepwood Road. Turn right and retrace your steps to Beith Town Centre.

Walk 5: Irvine to Dreghorn

Grade: C+ Distance: 4.5 miles & 4 miles Total 8.5 miles Paths & pavements

The walk starts at the War Memorial near Irvine Cross. (NS322388) There are various car parks in Irvine adjacent to the starting point of the walk.

1 Cross the road and walk along the Kirkgate down to the river. Turn left and take the riverside path. Follow the path till the end of the cemetery wall. The path veers to the left at St Innans Well. Go up the steps and turn right past Glebe Primary School into Golfields. There is an interesting building on the right which was the *Town Powder House. Keep to the path ignoring right and left turns, passing through trees, then down steps taking you under the main road. Keep to the path along the River Irvine then the Annick, bordering Tarryholme Park. The track passes under a footbridge, then a road bridge and arrives at the Irvine to Dreghorn Road. (NS330384)

2 Cross at the lights and rejoin the path, signposted Kilmarnock, which takes you round the hotel. Watch out for golf balls! Follow this track, keeping to the river until you come to the back of Greenwood Academy. You are now walking along the disused railway track. Keep on path following cycle path signs for Kilmarnock and cross a minor

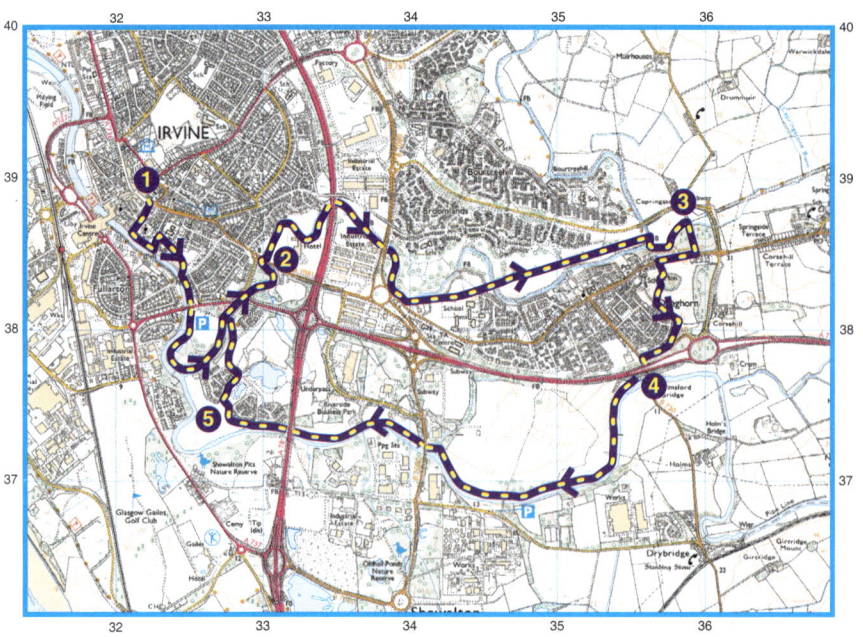

oad leading to cemetery, then a footbridge over river until you come to the locally amed Coach Brae. (NS359386)

At this juncture there are 3 alternatives:

1 continue on cycle path to Kilmarnock and return to Irvine by bus.

2 if you have walked far enough, turn right and take the bus back to the start.

3 continue the walk back to Irvine.

To continue the walk back to Irvine, turn right and take the path to the main road. Turn ight and walk on the pavement until you reach the Dreghorn signpost. There is an bvious path across the road, alongside the first house. Take this path up to the War Memorial. Take a breather on the benches and enjoy superb views of Ayrshire. Take the ath that goes down and around the perimeter of the houses, which will eventually lead o the B730 Dreghorn to Drybridge road just before the bridge. (NS356377)

Cross the road and take the path alongside the River Irvine. Keep walking on this path, o under a pipe bridge then pass a red bridge. When you arrive at the road bridge arrying the B7080 go up the steps away from the bridge and turn on to a faint isherman's path. Go over the fence and continue on this path passing two modern office locks on the right. The path passes under the A78 and is very overgrown in summer. At sign warning of erosion and unstable riverbanks, the path veers right and ends at pond n Tarryholme estate. (NS328375)

Go round the pond and arrive at the main road into the estate. Take a left and quick ight turn and walk as if you are leaving the estate. After a short distance you see houses n the left. Cross the road and take the path that runs alongside these houses. Cross the ridge facing you and continue on the path back to the steps under the main road. etrace your steps to Golfields, pass Glebe Primary School and enter the cemetery gates n front of you. On exiting the cemetery turn right and arrive back at the start of the valk.

see Walk 2 for details of the Powder House

Walk 6: Irvine Harbour & Beach Park

Grade: C   Distance: 5 miles   Pavements & paths

1 Start at the Town House. Cross the road and walk up the street facing, Kirkgate. After a few yards facing you is Puddleford Lane, known locally as the Puddly Doodly. Walk down the lane, down the steps and turn right onto a path alongside the River Irvine.

2 Go under the shopping mall and you are now in Low Green. Have a look at the Trade's Marker then onto a bridge. Cross the bridge and walk along the lane facing you. Go under the bridge, veer left, then turn right at the church hall. At the roundabout, go left. Take care using the paths to cross the road.

3 Go left past Ayrshire Metal Products and follow the road as it veers right into Montgomerie Street, leading to the harbour side. On the right is the Maritime Museum and this is a suitable point to start a short walk. Take a look at the bird board and enjoy the antics of the many birds resident in the mud flats of the River Irvine. Pass the statue of The Carter and his Horse and walk along the esplanade to the mouth of the river at the very end of a short peninsula. From this point, there are great views of Arran, Ailsa Craig and the Ayrshire coastline on a good day.

4 Retrace your steps to the roundabout at the harbourside car park, turn right onto the access road and then onto the path running parallel to the sea. Alternatively, stroll along the beach. Either way you will reach the Dragon Sculpture. Again, here are excellent views which you can enjoy while having a wee seat before heading away from the sea and along the ridge path. At the bottom of the steps turn left and head for the Magnum Leisure Centre, skirting the beach pond.

5 Retrace your steps back down the harbourside. Go under the railway bridge, turn right along path to pedestrian crossing at McDonalds and take path to the left alongside Marks & Spencer. At the roundabout, cross at the zebra crossing and pass between Annick and Afton Court where there is an opening onto the path. Turn right and follow the path to a bridge, which you cross and then turn left onto the Golfields. After passing Glebe School go through the small gate of the cemetery and on exiting, turn right to return to the start of the walk.

Low Green

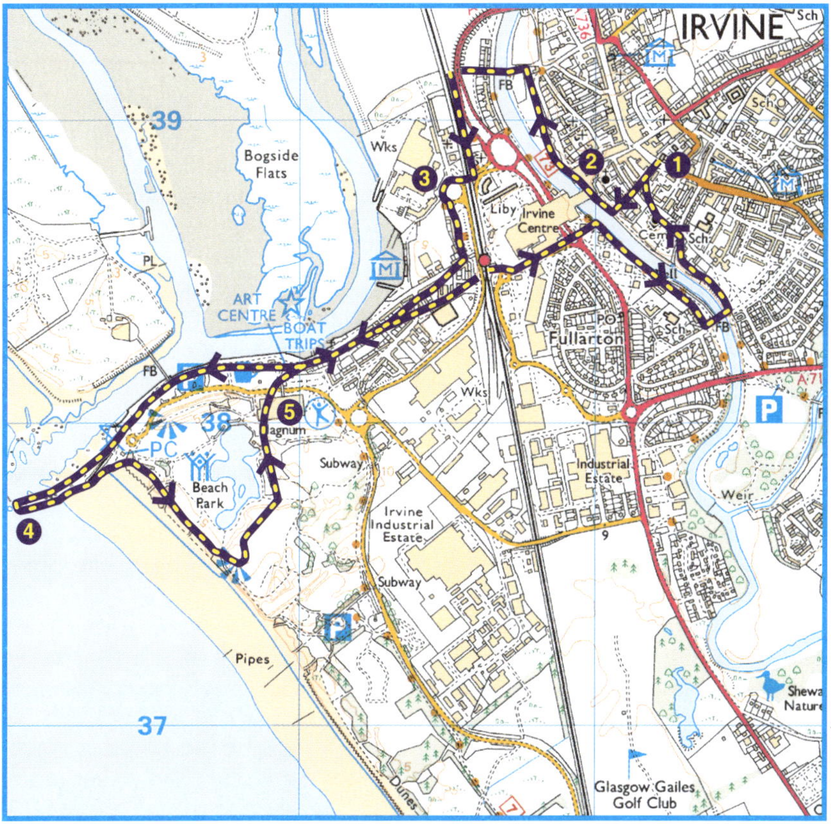

The Dragon Sculpture

Walk 7: Dreghorn to Eglinton Park

Grade: B Distance: 11miles THC 138 metres Paths, tracks & minor roads

Walk starts in Dreghorn. Park in small area opposite cemetery. (NS351383)

1 Cross road and follow New Town Trail as it curves right. Continue on path to T-junction at Coach Brae. Turn left and follow path through underpass to road veering right and leading to Perceton Row. Pass the row of houses and continue until you reach the junction with the main road. Extra care is required as there is no pavement for 1 mile. (NS353401)

2 Cross the Girdle Toll – Stewarton road, B769 and take the NoThrough Road to Kirkhill, picking up the pathway on left hand side of road. At the end of this section you will reach a road. Cross this road, turn left over River Annick Bridge (NS350405) and then immediately right.

3 Walk straight ahead past the large workshop until you come to the road in front of the hotel. Cross the road and go straight ahead with the hotel on the left. At the next road, past the woods, cross over, turn right and walk for 100 metres. Turn left onto path, walk for 50 metres then turn right. Go through underpass and make for Five Stanes Mound. (NS339414)

4 Follow the path over the Mound and down the other side. Take the narrow path veering right and continue straight ahead till you reach the loch. Go straight ahead and make a circuit of the loch. At the iron bridge cross over to the castle. (NS322421)

5 Follow the path to left of the castle making your way to the café and visitor centre. Leave the café area by crossing to the track, keeping the car and coach parks on the right Continue on this track, pass the underpass on the right and continue until you reach the stone Dovecote. At the Dovecote go right and cross the main road with care. (NS329415)

6 Go left for about 10 metres then turn right onto the narrow farm road. Follow this road round to the houses in Montgomerie Park. Go through the houses and take the path to the left leading to the main road. Cross the road at the pelican crossing. Keeping Earlswood Estate on the right, walk down towards the bridge, past the entrance to the houses at Pavilion Gardens on the right and the pond on the left. Cross the bridge (NS334404), turn right, then left and keep going ahead through the houses of the Stanecastle Estate. Keep to the path with the nursery on the right and continue along, keeping the roundabout on the left. Follow the path ahead and go left through the underpass. (NS335398)

7 Exit the underpass, turn left and walk for approximately 1/3 mile with the road on the left and factories on the right. You will come to a car park at the access road to an industrial estate. Go up the steps, cross the road and follow the path down to pass the

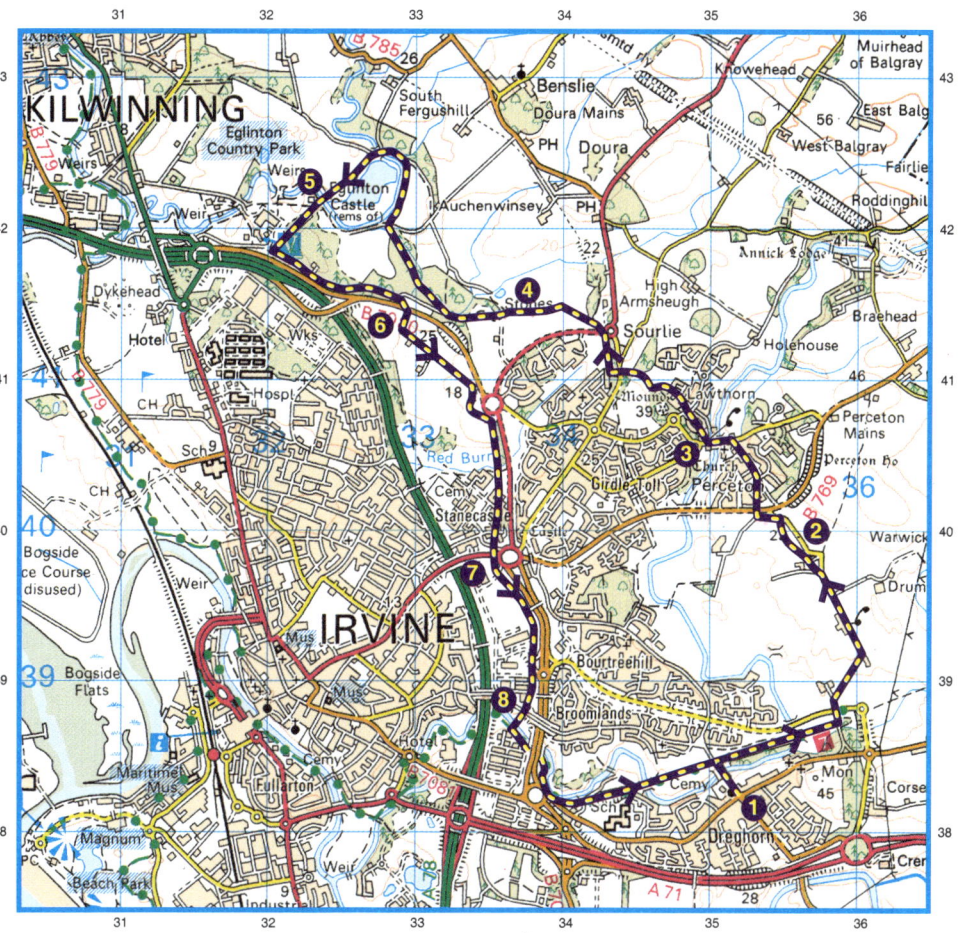

Wool Growers factory on the right. Keep going ahead on the trail through the factories and you eventually come to the bus route. (NS337387)

8 Cross the road and on to cross the bridge over the River Annick. Turn left and follow the New Town Trail along the river behind Greenwood Academy, then back to the car park.

Walk 8 : Stanecastle to Girdle Toll

Grade: C Distance: 5 miles or shorter version 2 miles Paths, tracks & pavements

There are parking bays at top end of main road in Girdle Toll past shops. Walk starts at Stanecastle Keep next to Stanecastle roundabout (NS337399)

1 Walk towards a footbridge over B769 but do not cross the bridge. Turn left and follow the path, which runs parallel to Middleton Road until you come to an underpass on the right. Go through the underpass and walk ahead for ¼ mile until you reach Bourtreehill Park. Go through the park past the swings on the right. When you reach the lane ahead, go left to the bottom of the lane then turn right. Soon you will come to the footbridge over the River Annick (NS347395)

For the shorter version: Go straight ahead and follow the path, looping back to the bridge. From here retrace the route back to Stanecastle Keep.

2 To do the longer walk, cross the bridge and proceed on a broad path till you reach a gate at a sort of mini T-junction (NS350397). Turn left then right. Continue until you reach Middleton Road. Cross the road, turn right and when you reach a small side road go left for a few yards and enter a wood on the right, via a wooden gate. Follow the path until you come to a gate. (NS354402) Go through and turn left into Perceton Wood. The woodland path is particularly pretty at springtime.

3 On reaching the housing estate, go left through the houses and then left again past the entrance to Perceton House. Continue ahead until you reach Kirkhill Church (NS351406). Turn left onto a little side road just before the church. Immediately after the cottages, turn right onto a concealed grassy track which curves round the side of the River Annick. At the end of this track, just before the bridge, go up steps onto the B769. (NS348401)

4 Turn right across the bridge and walk for a few yards until you see a track on the other side of the road. Cross over onto this track, curving right and walk ahead onto the New Town Trail. Turn left, walking ahead until you reach the lane, which led to the footbridge at the start of the walk. Go right onto the lane. Enter the park, pass the swings on the left, turn right and retrace your steps to the start of the walk.

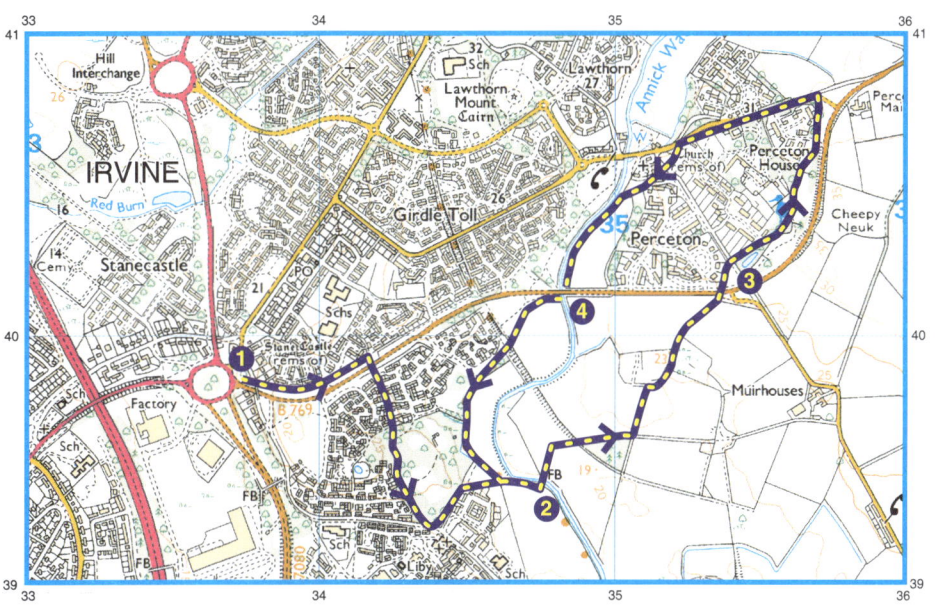

Stanecastle Keep

Walk 9: West Kilbride to Seamill

Grade: C Distance 5 miles, THC 146 metres Tracks, pavements & minor roads

The walk starts from the shore side car park off the A78 about 1 mile north of Ardrossan. (NS212453)

1 From the car park, cross the busy main road carefully into a narrow road, almost directly opposite, signposted Public Footpath to High Road Ardrossan. Follow this road up the steep hill, over a railway bridge and round the side of a farm. Veer right through a gate onto a grassy track and follow this to Meadowhead Farm. Go through the farm and up to the road. (NS216470)

2 Turn left and walk along minor road dropping down into West Kilbride. Turn right at T-junction into Meadowfoot Road and carry on over the railway line. Turn left following sign for Town Centre and walk on through shops till you come to Glen Road. (NS205483)

3 Turn left, walk down the road and enter Kirktonhall Glen. Watch out for the sleeping crocodile on the left and pause to enjoy The Hunterston Brooch Garden on the right. Keeping the Glen burn on the left, follow the path through the Glen until it emerges on to Glenbryde Road. Walk down the road until you come to the main A78 opposite the Seamill Hydro. (NS202471)

4 Cross the road and walk a short distance to the left. Just after the bus stop turn right and take footpath at gate down to the shore. Turn left and follow the shore side path back to the car park.

Around the 1830s a stunning brooch was found at Hunterston near the Goldenberry cliffs. Made around AD700, it is a highly accomplished casting of silver, richly mounted with gold, silver and amber decoration.

Hunterston Brooch Garden

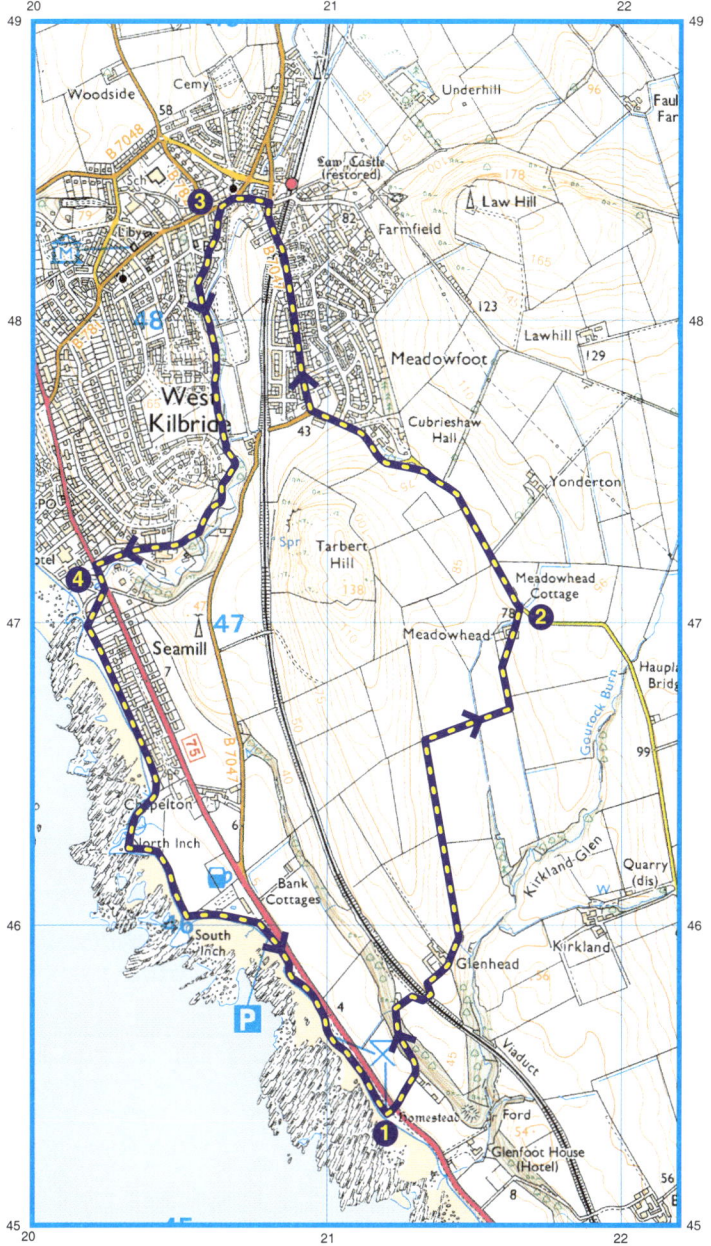

Walk 10: A Dauner* round Dalry

Grade: C+ Distance: 6 miles THC 194 metres Paths, pavements & minor roads

The walk starts at St Margaret's Church. (NS291494) There are two car parks in Dalry Town Centre.

1 From the church go up to the B780 Kilbirnie road junction. Turn right, walk for ½ mile and turn left immediately past Lomond Castings (do not cross the Rye Bridge.) (NS291502)

2 Very soon this track becomes a pleasant woodland path known locally as the Doggartland Walk (waymarked). Keep right at the next fork in the path. Note the old limekiln on the right at the padlocked gate. Bear left on the minor road and at the bridge look for a gap in the left wall. There are steps down to the burn for a pleasant coffee stop. The path joins the road just before Flashwood Farm. (NS277502)

3 At the road turn right. Follow the road, ignoring two minor roads on the right. Go past Baidland Mill to the right hand bend. Turn left onto the Velvet Path – there is a telegraph pole and a large boulder. (NS271502)

4 After ¼ mile you will come to a kissing gate on the right. Go through it entering Mosside 1. This and the next section are well signposted with white markers. At the path end, cross the road and enter Mosside 2. (NS281497). Cross the burn and continue on the path. Turn left at the junction passing under telegraph wires to reach wooden posts. Take either path to reach Morris Court Sheltered Housing. (NS289497)

5 Go along the side of the complex to the front, turn left and then right onto the main Kilbirnie road to take you back to Dalry town centre, where you can finish the walk. To extend the walk by a further 2.5 miles go straight along Roche Way. Cross the road at the pelican crossing and go along Vennel Street to reach the A737 Kilwinning Road. (NS289491)

6 At the road end turn right, cross the bridge then turn right again onto the B714 Saltcoats Road. Turn right at the traffic lights before bridge for the Lynn Glen car park. (NS287486)

7 Take the path that says 'No through road' passing between houses, one of which is Lynn House, the birthplace of local artist George Hamilton. Facing you is a kissing gate. Go through it and continue on the north bank of the Caaf Water passing a picturesque waterfall. At the head of the walk before a bridge is Peden's Pulpit named after the wandering Covenanting preacher. (NS282482)

8 On the homeward section there is a lade where the remains of a mill can be spotted. The walk continues on the south side of the glen, then retrace your steps back to the Dalry town Centre.

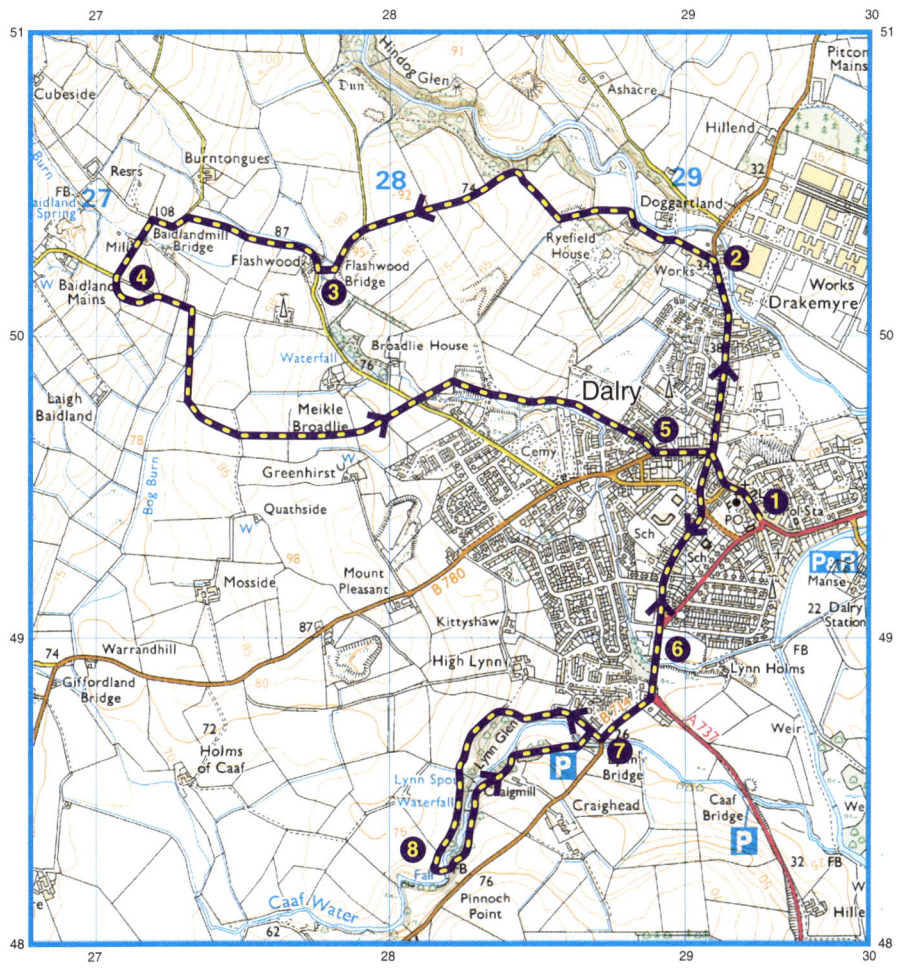

*Dauner: (Scots) stroll, wander, leisurely walk

Walk 11: Goldenberry Hill

Grade: B Distance: 10 miles, THC 248 metres Minor roads & tracks

Heading north on the A78 from Ardrossan the walk starts at the first shore side car park. (NS212453)

1 The walk starts on the beach walking towards Seamill going past caravan park, turning right onto grass path and following the shore line to the far end of West Kilbride Golf Course. (NS183485)

This first section is waymarked as part of the Ayrshire Coastal Path (which stretches from Glenapp to Skelmorlie.)

2 Turn right up path passing Kirkfield House to the road, then turn left down the road to Portencross Castle and picnic area. (NS176487)

3 Keep on the coastal path until just before Hunterston Power Station Main Block, turn right up the side of metal fence to gate, climb over the gate, turn left and go over the wire fence. Follow path along back of Power Station, keep on path through metal gate and carry on up the incline past the derelict building on right until you come to Goldenberry Cottage. Turn left and keep to the track until you come to metal gate on right, with two pylons opposite. (NS187510)

4 Go through gate, following track, then through another metal gate and keep on the track up to the mast and trig point at the top of the hill where you can enjoy the view. (NS183503)

5 Looking towards sea, go under the electric wire fence, turn left and make your way downhill to the track. Turn left following the track until you come to another metal gate. Climb over and carry on down to road at Ardneil Farm. (NS183487)

6 Cross over the road and go down to shore retracing your steps back to the car park.

Goldenberry Hill

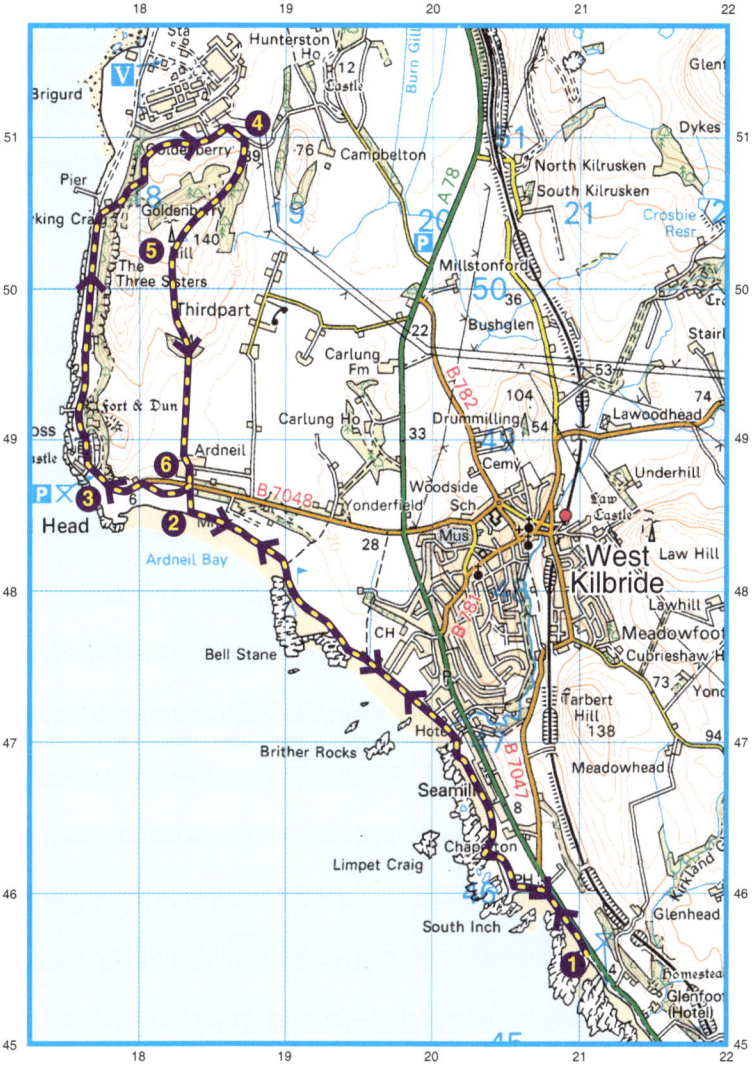

Walk 12 : North Hill

Grade: B+ Distance: 9 miles THC 421 metres Tracks & open ground

The walk starts from the shore side car park, off the A78 about 1 mile north of Ardrossan. (NS212453)

1 From the car park, cross the main road – take care – into a narrow road signposted Public Footpath To High Road Ardrossan. Follow this road up the steep hill, over a railway bridge and round the side of a farm. Veer right through a gate on to a grassy track and follow this to Meadowhead Farm. Go through the farm and up to the road. (NS216470)

2 Turn left and go along this road for about ¼ mile till you see a stile on the right and a sign, Footpath to Law Hill. Cross the stile and go up the hill between the line of trees to a road. On reaching the road turn right. In about 20 yards go over a stile on the left and follow the track up to Law Hill. At the top, as the track turns left towards a mast, turn right. Continue on along the side of the fence, through a gate and over the brow of a small hill, aligning your route with the left hand turbine. To the right of the trees there is a gate. Go through the gate and turn left. Go down the field and through the left hand gate on to a grassy track. This is an ancient coffin road. Turn right and follow this track past a small pond (not marked on map) where the track eventually turns left. (NS232484)

3 At this point, go straight ahead over some rough ground and through a gate. Once through the gate, veer right and head for the left hand side of a pylon and follow the power lines towards the next pylon. When about 100 yards from the second, turn right and climb North Hill to the mast. (NS238480) Ahead of you is Knock Jargon or Fort Hill surrounded by wind turbines.

4 From North Hill go downhill onto wind farm road. Continue down the road and, as it splits, go right curving round to walk parallel to the coast. Soon you will see a sign for Turbines 2, 3 & 4. Go up this road to Turbine 2. Go left at this turbine and make your way across a field, requiring some rough walking. Look out for a gap in the wall almost level with Turbine 2. Go over a fence, through wall. Turn right onto a grassy track cut between some fir trees. Follow the path uphill and round to the left. After a drop in the path, go right to take up the path which circles the pond and brings you back onto the coffin road at position 3.

5 Retrace your steps back to the road just beneath Law Hill. From here you you have two choices:

> *1* - turn right to extend the walk by walking down the road past Law Castle to West Kilbride and just after the road crosses the railway line, join Walk 9 at West Kilbride Town Centre, returning to the car park via Kirktonhall Glen and Seamill shore, or

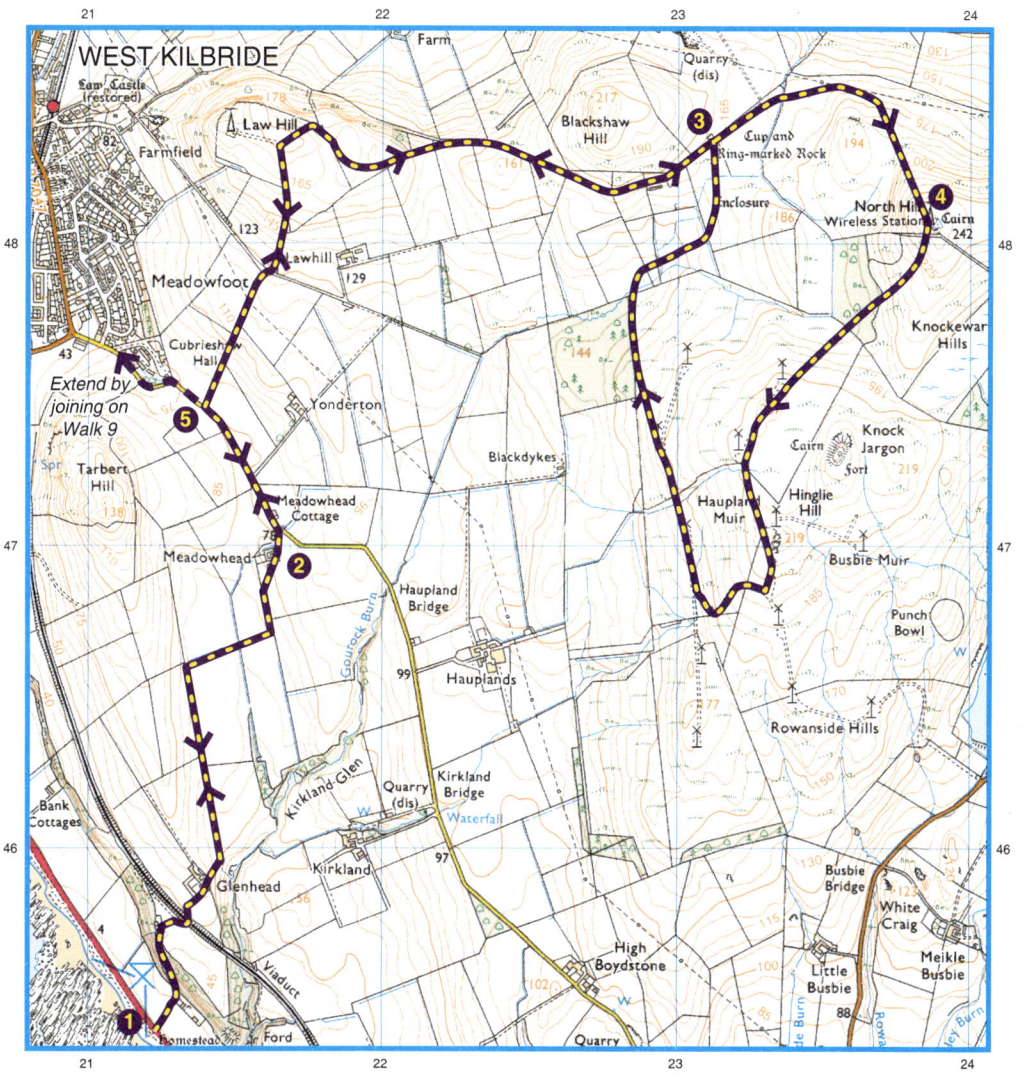

2 - go left in front of holiday homes back to footpath to Meadowhead Farm and retrace your steps back down the road to the car park.

Walk 13 : Kaim Hill

Grade: B+ Distance: 8 miles THC 481 metres Tracks & open moorland

The walk starts from Fairlie station car park (NS210546). There is a car park on the shore just off the A78 at the south end of Fairlie, a few minutes' walk from the station.

1 Start the walk by taking the path beside the last house, then turn right and walk in front of the little cottage facing the Fairlie Burn. Go over the railway bridge and follow the path through the woods until you reach Fairlie Castle. Continue up the steep path on the left of the burn, taking time to observe the many waterfalls along the way. When the rise levels out, cross over the stile on the left and follow the track round to the left across the small burn which leads into Fairlie Burn. (NS228545)

2 Cross to the stone dyke and fence on the right and follow this up towards Lairdside Hill. Go through the gate and head for the right end of the ridge to the right of Kaim Hill. Take care, as this part is especially rough and can be boggy. On the ridge, take the rough track along the top of the ridge (NS225540) towards Kaim Hill trig point.

3 Following the rough track, you find another track (NS224535) leading off to the left, up over a small hill. This takes you to Kaim Hill trig point (NS227534) where there can be spectacular views across the Clyde and to Knockendon Reservoir. Kaim Hill once had the highest production of millstones in Scotland and evidence of the quarrying can be seen on the south west side of the hill.

4 Retrace your steps back to rejoin the rough track. At the track turn left and follow this track down to the main road running through Fairlie Moor. Turn right at the road and follow it down past the road leading into Glenburn Reservoir. At the sign for the cattle grid follow the path to the left over to the hidden Glenburn Waterfall, which is a pleasant place for a stop (NS214522).

5 Retrace your steps back to the road. Cross this and go through the gate opposite. Follow the track with the trees to the left and Black Hill to the right. Carry on along the track for about 1 mile. At the end of the track, go over a stile at a gate, then after 20 yards, go through another gate on the left. Turn right and walk alongside a wall until you see a gate into the wood. Go through the gate and follow the broad track through the wood onto a narrow track slightly to the right. Continue until you reach a fence, climb over and cross the ford. Go left through the gate and cross the field going diagonally left, downhill to another gate. Go through this gate and turn right. Follow the edge of the field until you come to a kissing gate. Go through the gate and over the wooden bridge across Fairlie Burn. Turn left at the track and continue downhill to Fairlie Castle. Go onto the track behind the castle, down into the wood and over the railway bridge. Turn left after passing in front of the cottage into Fairlie Railway Station.

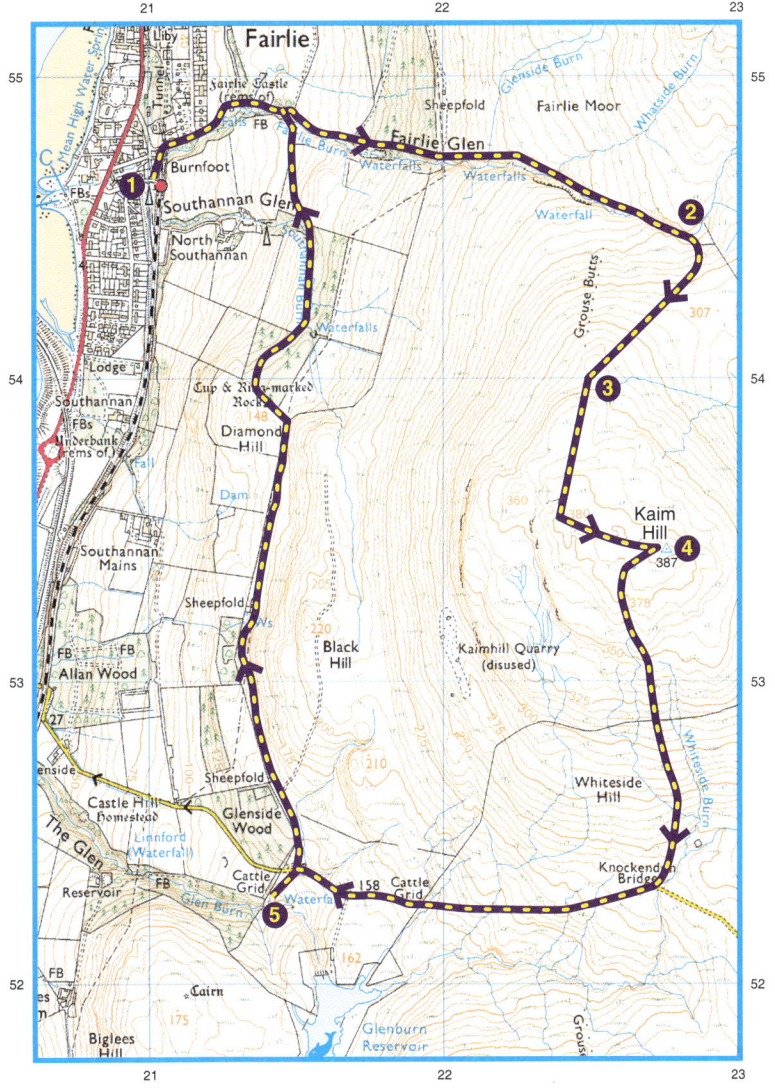

Walk 14 : Three Towns Walk

Grade: C+ Distance: 9 miles Good paths & pavements

Saltcoats, Stevenston and Ardrossan are known locally as the Three Towns. This walk starts at North Crescent Road at the west end of Ardrossan on the road to Seamill. Cars can be parked on the road. (NS228433)

1 Walk along North Crescent Road south towards Ardrossan: houses on left and the shore on right. The first 100 yards is a good cycle track then turns into a grassy track. Turn right through former petroleum complex, heading for a tall building, Ardrossan Pilot House straight ahead. On reaching the harbour, turn right and follow the path round to the Pilot House. (NS226423)

2 Carry on round with the houses on the left and harbour on the right until reaching an old, brown building. Leave the harbour here, turn left, passing the old Police Station on the left and turn right into Princes Street. Continue over the railway until you reach the shore promenade. Just at the start of the promenade there is a memorial to the crew of HMS Dasher. (NS232421)

3 Continue on the shore promenade for 2 miles, passing Saltcoats and heading towards Stevenston. At the end of the promenade, the path narrows and heads inland running alongside the railway. After a short distance, take the right fork and follow the path through the sand dunes onto the Stevenston shore access road. (NS269409)

4 Turn left into Stevenston, crossing railway line and turn left after the disused police station into Moorpark Road West. Continue along the road to a good path heading back towards Saltcoats with the golf course on the right. The path veers right to cross over the main road via a footbridge and Auchenharvie Academy is on the right. Follow a narrow tarmac path uphill, cross Kerr Street and continue for ½ mile, passing under bridges. The path ends at the last bridge. Walk straight on between houses until you reach a dead end. (NS244421)

5 Turn right, walk a few yards and turn left. There are playing fields on the right. Continue along the path until it meets some houses. Go right around Mitchell Place and cross over Caledonia Road into Holm Plantation Park. (NS240421)

6 Follow the path across the park into South Beach Road and turn left over the rail bridge at Ardrossan South Beach Station. Go downhill and turn right onto the main road. Take the second on the right and after about 100 yards, turn left onto a narrow path with the Bowling Club on the right. Continue along the track, turn right over the railway footbridge and uphill to the ruined castle. (NS233423)

7 Enjoy the views then go downhill at fence corner about 80 steps into Glasgow Street in Ardrossan. Turn right and cross road then turn left into Barr Street. Turn right at the Fire Station and follow road bearing left into North Crescent Road and back to start of walk.

Saltcoats - Stevenston Shoreline

Walk 15: Douglas Park

Grade: B+ Distance: 7 miles, THC 450 metres. Paths & open hillside

There are some steep sections on this walk, both up and down

From the seafront in Largs, drive up Nelson Street (St Columba's Parish Church with the clock in the steeple is on the corner). Turn right along Moorburn Road at the very top, then left up Flatt Road. Go past Largs Academy, cross Eastern Avenue into Bellsdale Avenue and park past the last house at the top of the avenue. (NS211593).

1 Start the walk by going along the track into the woods beside the Gogo Water. At the bridge in the middle of the woods, cross the Water, turn right and go up the narrow path. When you come to the end of this path, turn hard left up to the fence at the top and go over it. Go through the larger fence ahead of you and keep walking until you reach the large tree ahead. Then, climb up to the right and walk through gorse bushes where there is a sheep track. Keep on until you reach the road (NS212586).

2 Turn right until you reach the steps at Douglas Park. Turn left, go up the steps and follow the path up beside the wall until it turns right, going up to the viewpoint. (NS214585). The views here can be marvelous and do take time out to enjoy them.

3 From the view point, head into the hills following the clear track until you reach a wall with barbed wire on top. Just beside the wall, slightly to the right, you will see the first of three cairns. Look ahead up to the hill and you will see the second cairn. Head for the second cairn. From here, follow the track to the third cairn and walk on until you are about 50 yards from the wall ahead. Then, carefully make your way down the steep hillside to the old bridge. The bridge is in an unsafe state, so either find stepping stones or a narrow section to cross the Gogo Water. (NS233593)

4 Once across, make your way up to the top of the incline and follow the wall straight up until you come to a gate. Go through it and turn left. This track will take you to Greeto Bridge (NS228597). This is a pleasant spot to linger and rest after your exertions. From here follow the track down to the start of the walk.

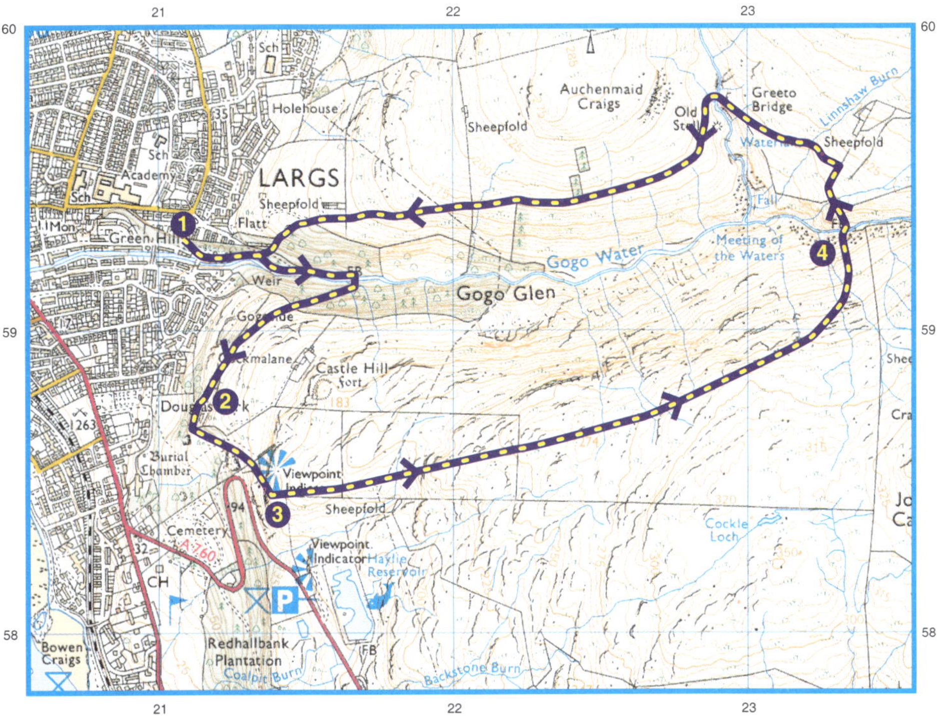

A frozen section of Gogo Water

Walk 16: Rowantree Hill

Grade: B+ Distance: 9 miles, THC 450 metres Paths & open hillside

This walk is challenging and requires experience.

The walk starts from a path leading from Bellsdale Avenue in Largs. From the seafront in Largs, drive up Nelson Street (St Columba's Parish Church with the clock in the steeple is on the corner). Turn right along Moorburn Road at the very top then left up Flatt Road. Go past Largs Academy, cross Eastern Avenue into Bellsdale Avenue and park past the last house at the top of the avenue. (NS211593)

1 Go back down the road for 100 yards and take signposted path on the right. Go over the stile and follow the tarmac road. Continue to another stile which leads to a grassy track which leads to one further stile. Continue along to a signposted path on the left. (NS227595)

2 This will lead you to Auchenmaid Crags then to the left and around up to the masts. (NS224599)

3 Follow the fence down towards the sea until you come to a gate. (NS223599) Go through the gate and onto a clear track which will take you past the side of Wooy Hill, which has a small cairn. Follow the track to Langley Hill. (NS232611)

4 Beyond Langley Hill the path becomes faint after passing through a gate but the track soon becomes clearer as it swings left and then up to the right towards Girtley Hill. On the approach to the hill, the path runs up to a wall and fence. The best place to climb over is where two iron bars are sticking up. (NS233614) After a short distance, you arrive at the cairn on Girtley Hill.

5 You now have to cross Bessel Moor heading due north for ½ mile, aiming for a small cairn with a stony cut-out on the hill beneath it, just beyond a fence. (NS232620) Go north east for 2/3 of a mile towards another stony section with a fence in front of it. Rowantree Hill is in front of you. (NS239629). From here, you should be able to see the trig point on Burnt Hill diagonally to the right. The views are excellent on a good day. The stony area just beneath the top is a good spot for a well-earned break.

6. To return, retrace your steps back to the top of Girtley Hill and take the track over Langley and Wooy Hills back to the gate, down from the masts. (NS223599)

7. Go through the gate and turn right along the track until you reach the track above Gogo Glen. (NS221594) Turn right onto this, go over the stile and down to the car park at Bellsdale.

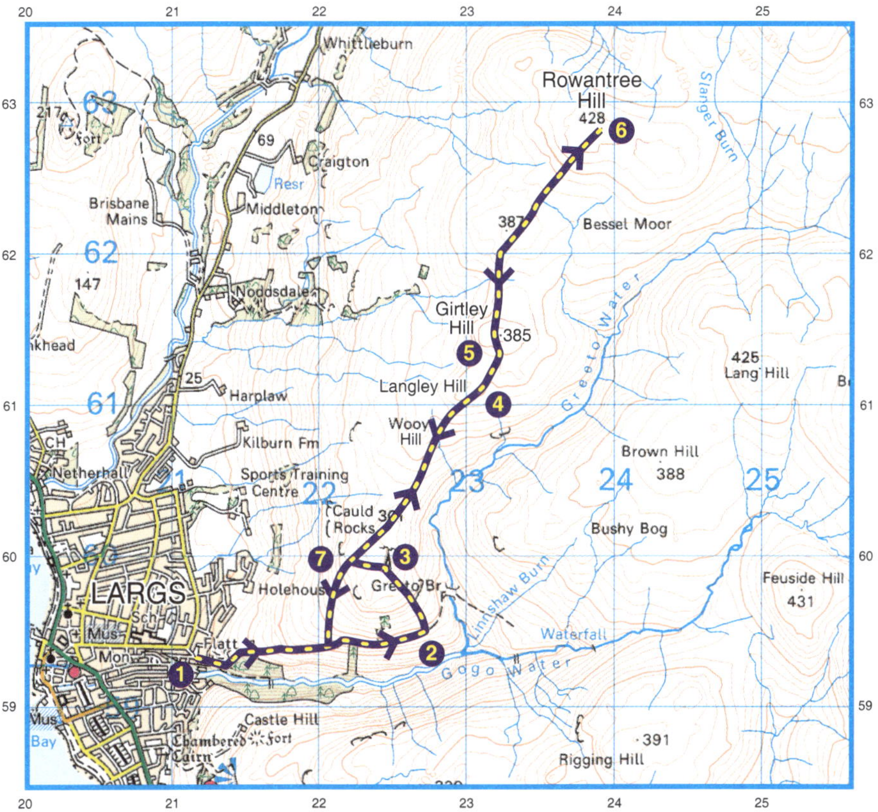

Snowdrops in Gogo Glen

Walk 17 : Blaeloch

Grade: B+ Distance: 7 miles, THC 450m Indistinct paths & open hillside
Recommended time: between October and May

The walk starts at Fairlie Station car park (NS210546). (For parking see Walk 13)

1 Start the walk by taking the path beside the last house, then turn right and walk in front of the little cottage facing the Fairlie Burn. Go over the railway bridge and follow the path through the woods until you reach Fairlie Castle. (NS213549)

2 From the Castle, follow the path up Fairlie Glen passing a sign that directs you to a waterfall which is worthwhile diverting to view. Come back and take the path signposted To The Moor. After a steep climb, go over a stile (NS220547) and slightly further on, a second stile will lead you onto the open hillside. Follow this path till you see a sign for Kaim Hill. At this point, veer left, and head for a group of rocks - a favourite Cunninghame Rambler's coffee stop. (NS229547)

3 Climb above these rocks and look for the ruined sheepfold on the left. Take the track on the right hand side of Outermoor Burn, passing the single tree and keeping high. Head east and walk until you see the Wind Farm in the distance. Then turn left and head for the first cairn. From the rise past the tree to the cairn should take approx. 20 minutes. (NS239548)

4 From the cairn, keep going north east towards some rocks and a small hill in the distance. You soon pass the aircraft wreckage on the left. The aircraft was a Firefly DT977 a member of 1772 Squadron. It crashed on 26th October 1944, with no record of casualties.

After approximately 10 minutes, you will see Blaeloch Hill appearing on the left. Climb the small hill ahead and walk for another 10 minutes until you reach the second cairn. Now turn left, keeping high and walk for about 15 minutes until you see a small green patch below on the right. Head for this and from there, go through the old posts ahead, cross the small burn and keeping up, walk parallel to the Clea Burn. Keep going until you see the wall. (NS234569)

5 At the wall, turn left, go through wooden gate, cross the ford and start to walk beside the wall of Kelburn Estate. Keep walking until you reach a fork and take the lower track, keeping the wall in sight on the right. When the path appears to peter out at the disused quarry, go left and follow the line of telegraph poles. Go through a gate, across a burn and when you reach the end of the wall, go through the rickety gate. Turn right and you find yourself back at the first stile you climbed over at the beginning of the walk. Retrace your steps back to the castle, through the woods, past the cottages and back to the car park.

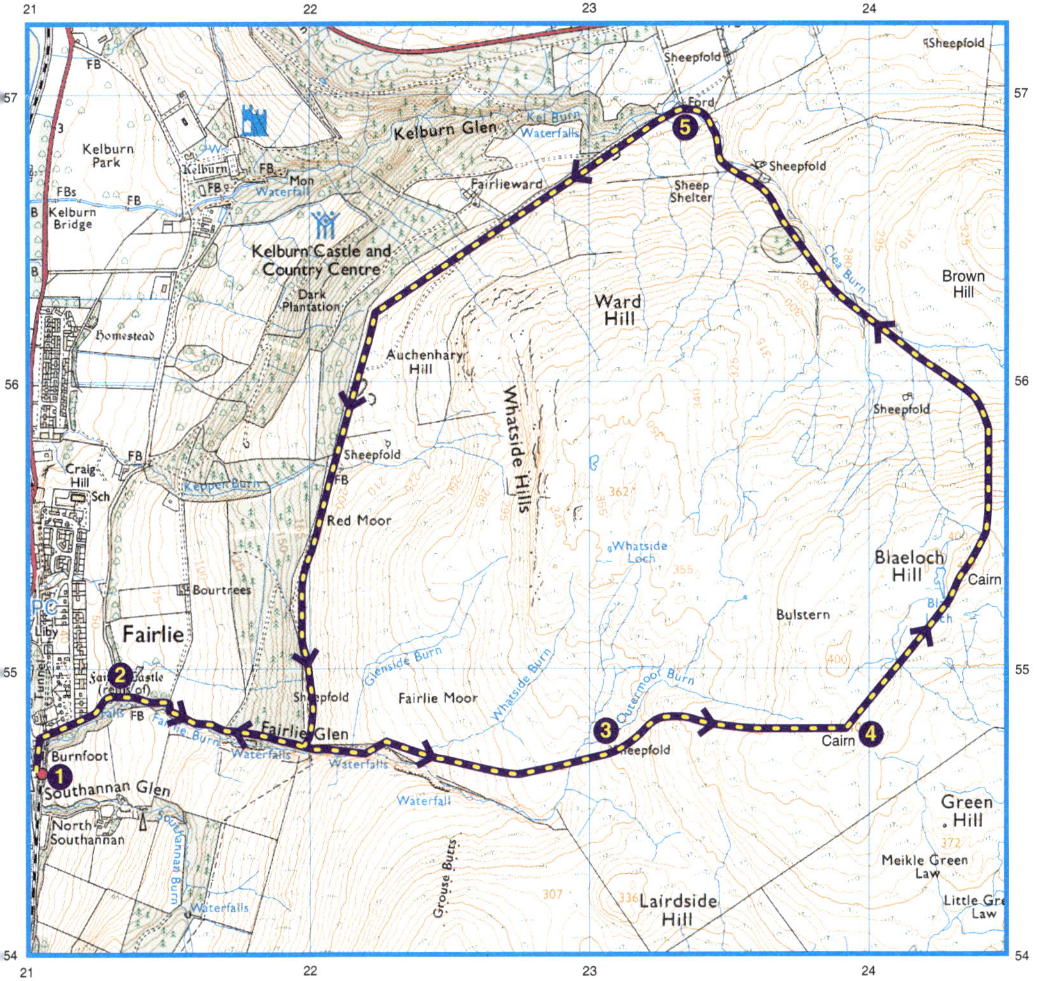

Kelburn Park
Kelburn Bridge
Kelburn
Mon Waterfall
Kelburn Glen
Kel Burn
Waterfalls
Fairlieward
Kelburn Castle and Country Centre
Dark Plantation
Homestead
Auchenhary Hill
Ward Hill
Whatside Hills
Sheepfold
Sheep Shelter
Ford
Clea Burn
Brown Hill
Craig Hill
Sch
Keppen Burn
Red Moor
Whatside Loch
Blaeloch Hill
Cairn
Bulstern
Bourtrees
Fairlie
Glenside Burn
Whatside Burn
Outermoor Burn
Fairlie Moor
Fairlie Glen
Fairlie Burn
Burnfoot
Southannan Glen
North Southannan
Southannan Burn
Waterfall
Grouse Butts
Green Hill
Meikle Green Law
Little Green Law
Lairdside Hill

Walk 18 : Ladyland to Cockston

Grade: B Distance: 8 miles, THC 346 metres   Minor roads, paths & tracks

Park in Kilbirnie town centre. The walk starts at the roundabout at the junction of the A760 and the B780. (NS316546)

1 Walk along the A760 towards Lochwinnoch and after a short distance turn right into a cul de sac off Stoneyholm Road. Go down the road to access the cycle path. Turn left on the cycle path signposted Lochwinnoch/Glasgow. Continue on the cycle path, crossing over a minor road (NS328555) and continue along, crossing over the Maich Water. About ½ mile after the Maich Water bridge, leave the cycle path on the ramp on the right up to a minor road. (NS334568)

2 Turn left on minor road and take in the views over Beith on a good day. Continue past Langslie Cattery, pass under the pylons (watching out for geese and ducks crossing the road!) carry on to the T-junction. (NS326577)

3 Turn left, cross over Maich Water and turn right into Ladyland House. Take the right fork away from the house going past the old stable block and carry on uphill on a stony track. The track bears left past the whitewashed Cockston Farm. Go through the farmyard, through the gate and turn right over the ford, following the grassy track until you reach Kilbanes Burn. (NS317592) Cross with care.

4 Continue along the grassy track and note the remains of settlement on skyline ahead – bending sharply to the right heading down to the footbridge over the Maich Water. (NS319596)

5 From the bridge, follow the track up a short distance to meet another track. Turn right and follow a faint path, which follows a line between gorse bushes on the left and a rocky outcrop on the right, heading down through boggy ground to a gate at a junction of walls. (NS324589)

6 Go through the gate and climb over the wall to go downhill between the walls. As the path improves, you see the former estate curling pond down on the left and soon you will pass the Maich Fishery on your right. Go over the stile and follow track down to road.

Turn right and right again at the next junction to join the road you came up on. This time, go past Ladyland House and continue down the "Dipple" Road, passing Redheugh Court (formerly a Salvation Army hostel) and a footbridge over the River Garnock, known locally as the Stock Bridge. Turn right onto the A760 and head back to Kilbirnie Town Centre.

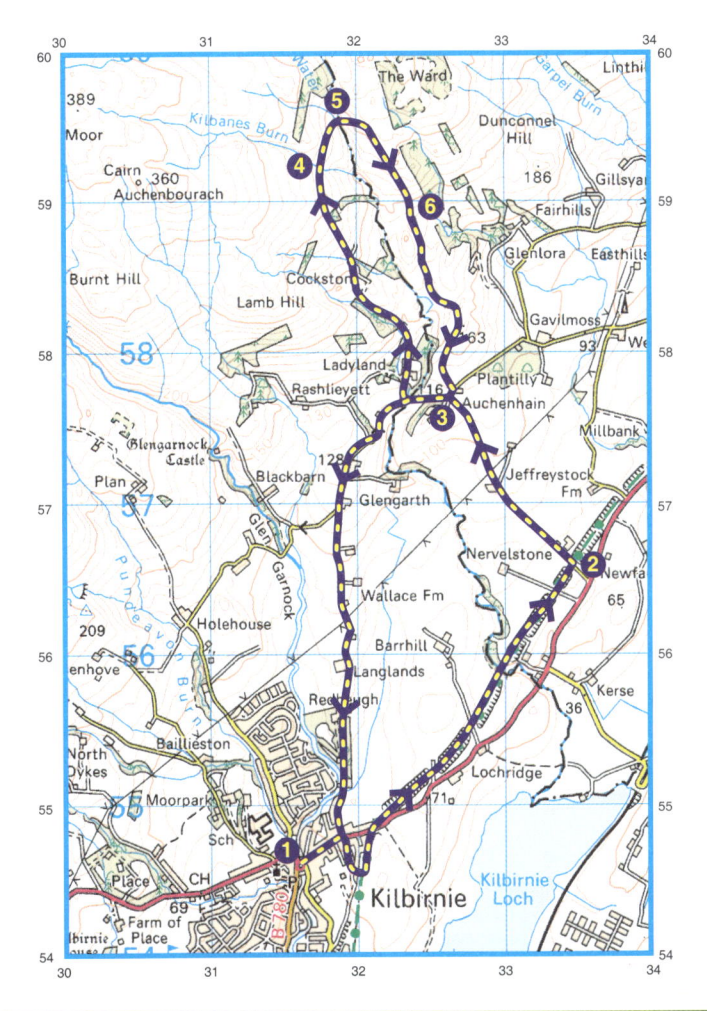

Rush Hour in the Garnock Valley!

39

Walk 19 : Irish Law

Grade: B+ Distance: 8 miles THC 529 metres Tracks & open moorland, a tough walk

Park at the Haylie Brae picnic site, which is on the A760 Largs to Kilbirnie road. The picnic site is approximately 1½ kilometres from the junction of the A78 trunk road and the A760. (NS215581)

1 Follow the gravel path uphill to the viewpoint. From here you can enjoy a panoramic view of the islands in the Clyde. Go through the kissing gate and follow the obvious path downhill. Cross bridge to meet a track and turn right onto this. Continue on this track and the remains of an old stone dyke on the right become apparent. Keep on the track until you come to a sheep enclosure. (NS218584)

2 From the enclosure, follow the wall running steeply uphill. Keep the wall to the left until you reach an electric fence. (NS222584) Go through gate and continue steeply uphill keeping the wall to the left. When you are opposite the masts above Auchenmaid Craigs, veer slightly away from the wall but keep it in sight. Continue until you reach Cockle Loch then pass between the wall and Cockle Loch, avoiding any boggy ground and continue towards a junction of walls ahead. Before reaching the junction, go through gate on the left and head diagonally to go through obvious gap in the wall and Jock's Castle should be directly in front. (NS236585)

3 From the summit pick up a track that runs in a NE direction to Little Craigstewart. Climb a little up Little Craigstewart looking for a track that runs to the right around its slope. This track should take you between Little Craigstewart and Cochrane's Crags. (NS240586) Keep going straight and Irish Law looms ahead of you. Keep going towards it using any sheep-trod path that will help your progress. If you go too far right you will meet a fence, stay this side of it and continue towards Irish Law. Cross the hard core track that comes up from Blairpark Farm and head downhill towards Irish Law. Cross a burn (NS251589) and then cross the Rye Water Head where the dry stone dyke becomes a fence. (NS252589) Follow the obvious track on the left to the summit. There are a few ways to reach summit of Irish Law from Rye Water Head, some easier than others.

4 Head downhill from Irish Law in a northerly direction and you will come to the wreckage of an aircraft (NS261592) between Irish Law and Little Irish Law. Leave the wreck site in a westerly direction, heading towards the track coming from Blairpark Farm and, again, cross the Rye Water Head (NS254591). Contour around Feuside Hill and head for the Blairpark Farm track just below the summit of Paton's Hill. Turn right on to this track and contour around Paton's Hill. This track will run out but continue on any sheep-trod path that you find, contouring around Mount Stewart, at times passing through some dense reeds but always keeping the Gogo Water on the right hand side. After passing Mount Stewart descend and head towards a wall. Look for a small kink in the wall (NS235590) where it crosses a burn and a few yards further upstream, there are the ruins of a gate. From the gate, head for a hilltop cairn, 245 degrees on your compass. Go through the gate and aim to the right to join a grassy ridge, which climbs to the hill via a sheep-trod path and then a track in a circuitous fashion. At the cairn (NS230587). there is an old track heading south to a cairn and a less obvious track heading west to another cairn on a hilltop. Take the track heading west, which soon broadens out to a wide, pleasant grassy track taking you to the next hilltop cairn. (NS222587).

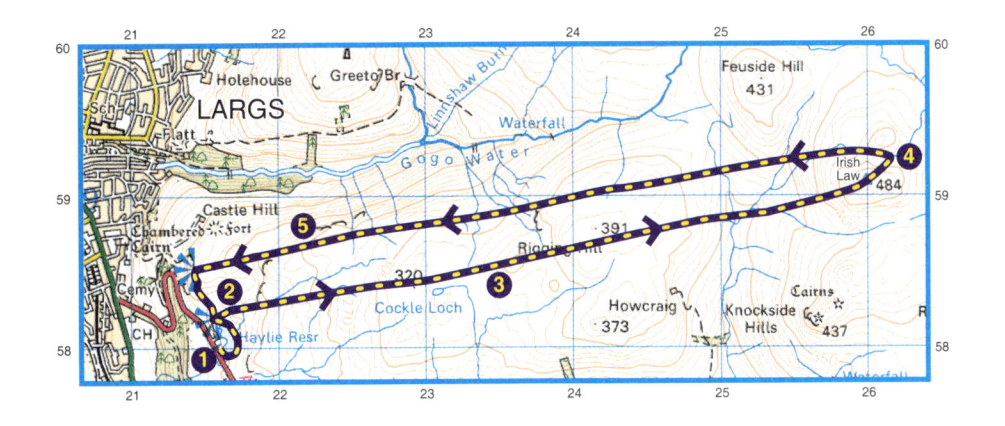

5 At this cairn, there are two tracks and another track heading towards a fence. Take the track heading towards the fence, cross the fence and keep following the track downhill. Pass between two rock outcrops and you will arrive at another cairn. (NS217585) Keep on the track and pass through a gap in a stone dyke wall. Keep on this track, going slightly uphill and from there you will be able to see another viewpoint indicator, benches and another cairn. Turn to the left (south) and follow the path downhill, which will soon join up with the outward path back to the car park.

The B.E.A. Viking G – AIVE crashed on the 21st April 1948. Captain John Ramsden failed to find the let-down beacon for Renfrew Airport. In attempting to regain the guiding beam, the aircraft hit the hillside after encountering severe turbulence in mist. The four crew and sixteen passengers had a miraculous escape, as the fuselage exploded shortly after the aircraft came to rest. Two engines and some tail and wing sections are the principal remains on site.

Walk 20: Crosbie Hills Linear

Grade: B   8 miles, THC 441 metres   Minor roads & tracks

The walk starts at West Kilbride station. (NS208484) Park at the station at weekends or at the small car park at the corner of Main Street/Gateside Street.

1 At the station, go right along Cubrieshaw Street towards the road to Dalry, the B781. Go left where the road forks, heading towards Crosbie Towers. After a short distance, take a narrow road on the right, leading to a caravan site. At the entrance to the site, take the left fork up past Crosbie Mains Farm. Keep going ahead past Crosbie Reservoir. As you approach cottage on the right, turn left through a gate. (NS221506)

2 Facing ahead, turn diagonally to your right and see a green patch on the side of Caldron Hill. Make for this by going right through a heathery path and then curving left towards a sheepfold (indistinct). At the near side of the sheepfold, start to make your way uphill over the green patch and then left to reach a substantial cairn on the top of Caldron Hill. This part is rough going as there is no path. The cairn is a good place to stop for time to catch your breath and, on a clear day, enjoy the excellent panoramic views. (NS228511)

3 Continue ahead for a short time and just after a dip in the terrain, you will see a track on the left going downhill to join another track which crosses the flat, wet ground in front of you. Cross over here to pick up another track, which runs along the bottom of the hill ahead of you. Go left on this track towards the coast, then after a short distance look for a "table" stone at the side of the track. Just past this, go right uphill following a track across the top of Glentane Hill. Keep going until you reach the Fairlie-Dalry Moor road. (NS216522)

4 Turn left and walk down the road until you reach a pronounced cut on your right where you turn left onto a grassy track to reach a scenic picnic spot by the waterfall. Retrace your steps back to the road. Cross over and go up a path at the left hand side of the cut out. Walk for about 5 minutes and just before the end of the trees, look for a path going uphill to the right. Walk up for about 60 metres and turn left onto a track going across the top of Black Hill. (NS215531)

5 Follow this track and just before you reach a wall, descend to the lower track on your left. Go over a stile at a gate, turn immediately left, then through another gate. Turn right and walk alongside a wall until you reach a gate into the wood. Go through the gate and follow the broad track through the wood onto a narrow track, slightly to the right. Continue until you reach a fence, climb over and cross the ford. Go left through gate, cross the field going diagonally left to another gate. Go through this gate and turn right. Follow edge of field till you come to kissing gate. Go through and over wooden bridge across Fairlie Burn. (NS213549)

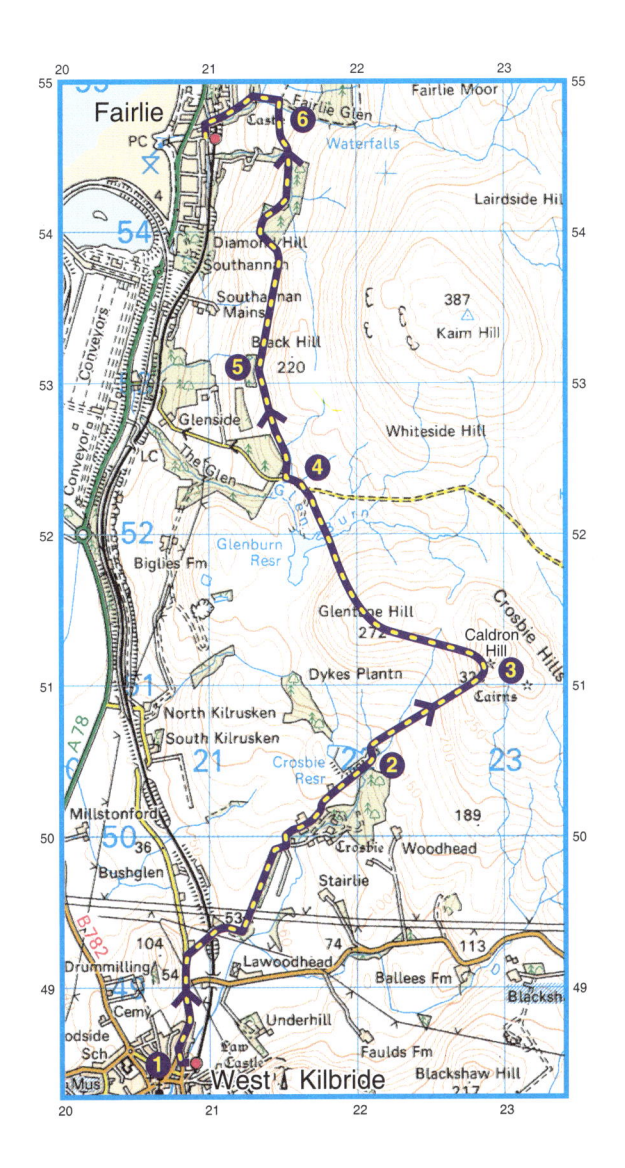

6 Turn left at track and continue downhill to Fairlie Castle. Go onto the track behind the Castle, down into the wood and over the railway bridge. Turn left after passing in front of a cottage into Fairlie Railway Station. Return to West Kilbride by train (one per hour) or by 585 bus (two per hour) from the main road.

Walk 21: Glaid Stone Hill

Grade: C Distance: 7.2 miles, reaching 127metres Generally quiet country roads

The Isle of Cumbrae is reached by car ferries, which run regularly from Largs pier (NS202595) Largs is well served by bus and rail transport and has adequate car parking.

1 The walk starts at the ferry slip on the Isle of Cumbrae.(NS184586). From the slip turn left towards the Sportscotland National Centre Cumbrae. Pass this and turn right after a whitewashed cottage on the corner of a road signposted Inner Circuit Walk. This is Ferry Road and was the original road to Millport before construction of the shore road.

2 Continue on this road for ¾ of a mile to a junction sign posted Millport via Glaid Stone Hill. Turn right and follow this road to the top of the hill where you will see a trig point and a viewpoint. This is the highest point on the island with excellent views on a clear day. (NS167570)

3 From the viewpoint, return to the road and turn right, passing through Breakough Farm (NS165556) to a junction at the bottom of the hill. Turn right here into a road signposted Millport Direct 1/3 mile and follow this road to Millport. It is worth stopping to visit the stunning Cathedral of The Isles (the smallest cathedral in Britain and one of Scotland's architectural gems) and its grounds which you pass on the left.

4 When you reach the shore road, turn left and continue along until you the road bends to the right round Kames Bay. (NS170552). Do not turn right, but go straight ahead into Ferry Road. Continue on this road back to the ferry slip.

Millport

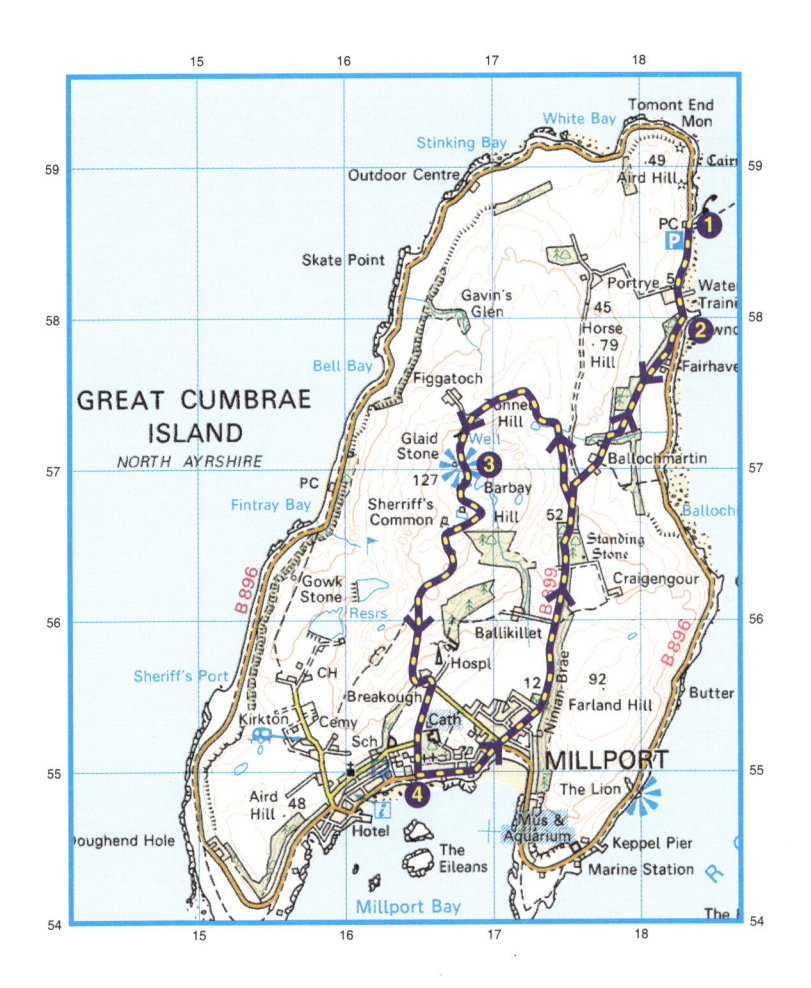

Great Cumbrae, Little Cumbrae, Bute & Arran from Largs Hills

45

Walk 22 : Glenashdale Falls

Grade: C+ Distance: 5 miles, THC 148 metres Tracks & minor roads

The ferry from Ardrossan lands at Brodick, so you must first travel 8 miles along the main road, south to Whiting Bay. This is a beautiful walk especially after rain, as the falls will be exceptionally full. The walk starts at Whiting Bay village centre car park. (NS045262)

1 Walk along the shore road pavement heading south for about a third of a mile until you reach the access road to the golf course. (NS046256)

2 Turn right and follow the signpost to Glenashdale Falls. Follow the track and go through a gate until you see the forest ahead. Pass through another gate into the forest, cross the stream and follow the signs. It is worthwhile diverting off the main path to view the falls from different angles at the designated viewpoints. At the top of the falls, picnic tables have been placed so that walkers can have lunch. Unfortunately, midges abound! (NS029249)

Glenashdale Falls

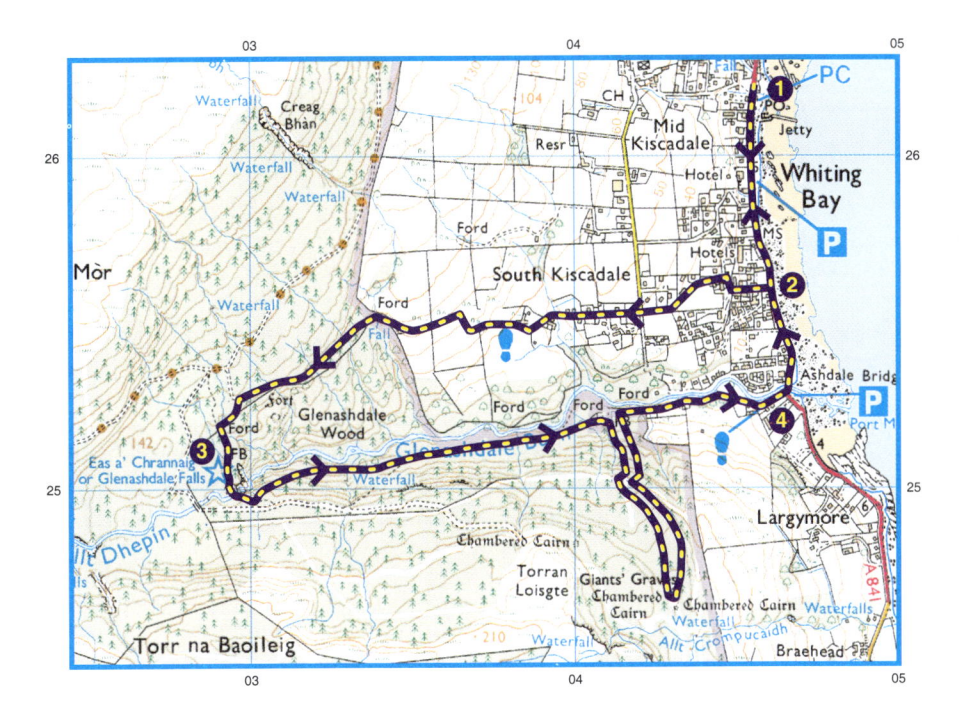

3 To make the walk circular, you cross the top of the falls and descend the south side of the Glenashdale Burn. Three quarters of the way down, signs will direct you to Giant's Graves, which are ruins of chambered tombs thought to date from between 3000 and 2000 BC and worth a visit, although a steep climb.

4 When you return to the main path, continue down towards Whiting Bay, pass the cottages and you will soon reach the main road again. Turn left and walk on until you arrive at the car park where you started the walk.

Walk 23 : Bridges & Burns in Arran

Grade: C+ Distance: 6.5 miles THC 249 metres Way-marked paths

The walk starts at the Ranger Centre in the grounds of Brodick Castle. A bus service runs from Brodick pier to the car park at Brodick Castle. (NS017380)

1 Leave the car park and turn left on to the perimeter road. After a short distance, you will see the Ranger Centre on the right. Ahead of you is a path signposted Woodland Walk. There is a board here with signs to Goatfell. Cross the stile onto the Millburn Trail. Follow the blue signs with the next point of interest being the Hamilton Cemetery on the left among the trees. Keep to the Goatfell path till you reach a right turn signposted Balmoral Ride. (NS006384)

2 Take regular stops on the Balmoral Ride to admire the views. Keep to the Ride ignoring right and left turns until you arrive at Merkland Burn. Go over the bridge and turn right and take the obvious path down the side of the burn. On reaching the end of the path, turn left onto wide track. After a short distance you will see Dan's Walk on the right. This is a short detour through ancient trees, sculptures and a raised beach. Keep to the path going over a bridge and up and down steps. At a post with a green arrow is the first of the sculptures. A point of interest is the overhanging rock feature which is a raised beach. (NS026387)

3 Go round the left side, taking the path with the other sculptures. Look out for red squirrels. You will rejoin the path you left. Turn left, walk down towards the main road. Just before the road, take a track off to the right, Lady Mary's Trail. This will take you back to the castle car park.

4 Pass alongside the castle and take the pedestrian exit. You will see a path on your left. Take this path to the sawmill. Cross the main road to the coast, cross the bridge, turn right and follow the coastal path to Brodick.

Sculptures at Dan's Walk, Brodick Castle

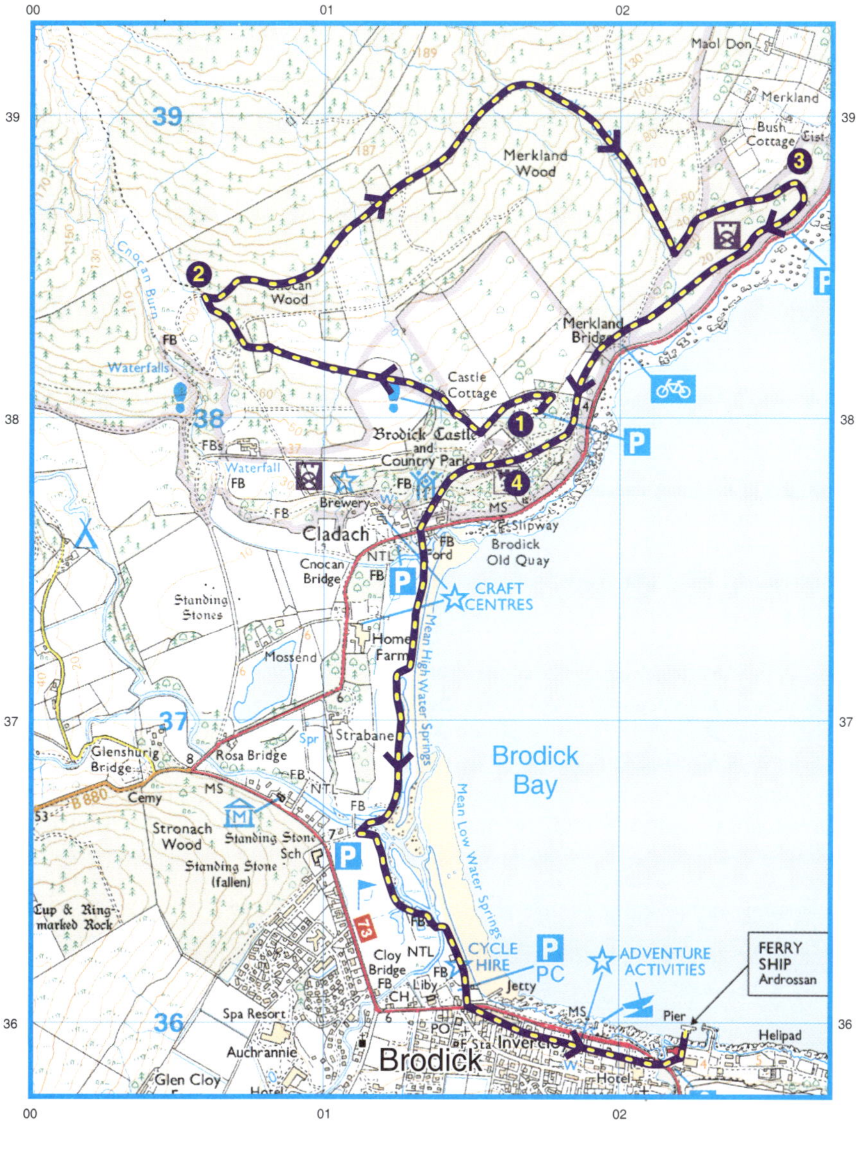
Maol Don
Merkland
Bush Cottage
Merkland Wood
Cnocan Wood
Cnocan Burn
Waterfalls
Merkland Bridge
Castle Cottage
Brodick Castle and Country Park
Waterfall
Brewery
Cladach
Slipway
Brodick Old Quay
Cnocan Bridge
CRAFT CENTRES
Standing Stones
Home Farm
Mossend
Mean High Water Springs
Strabane
Brodick Bay
Glenshurig Bridge
Rosa Bridge
Cemy
Stronach Wood
Standing Stone
Standing Stone (fallen)
Cup & Ring-marked Rock
Mean Low Water Springs
Cloy Bridge
CYCLE HIRE
Jetty
ADVENTURE ACTIVITIES
FERRY SHIP Ardrossan
Pier
Helipad
Spa Resort
Auchrannie
Brodick
Glen Cloy
Hotel

Walk 24 : Cock of Arran

Grade: B   Distance: 7.2 miles, THC 445 metres   Minor roads & tracks

Take the bus to Lochranza or park at the pier. Start the walk at St Bride's Parish Church. (NR937502)

1 Cross the road and to the left after a few yards, a lane is signposted The Cock of Arran. Follow the lane past the golf course then turn right, signposted Laggan, onto a road that gradually gains height, passing cottages on the way. Higher up, join a track to the left, signposted To the Cock and Laggan. (NR945501)

2 Proceed along this track crossing an old wooden footbridge over a burn and then start the long but gradual climb to the highest point of the walk. At the top the views to Bute, The Cowal peninsula and the mainland are outstanding. Walk down the grassy track to the pretty whitewashed cottage at Laggan. (NR978508)

3 From the cottage, the path bears left, heading North. It is signposted with the blue arrow logo of the Arran Coastal Path. Running close to the shore, the track goes across some boggy ground, passes through a gap in a stone wall, then continues across the grassy foreshore. The path goes past the famous Cock of Arran: a large sandstone block that has long lost its head. (NR956522)

4 The way becomes more challenging at the foot of the cliffs, wending its way around and over fallen boulders made of very rough conglomerate. There is an alternative path through the trees. On either route, care must be taken. Eventually, you drop down to a shingle shore and the first cottages appear on the approach to Lochranza. The walk continues along one of Arran's raised shorelines turning the corner into Lochranza. The track passes the first cottages then swings round to the north shore of Lochranza. Now on the final leg join the tarmac road at a row of houses. (NR932513)

5 Continue on to rejoin the lane that runs by the golf course. If you have time, visit the dramatic ruin of Lochranza Castle, parts of which date back to the 14th Century.

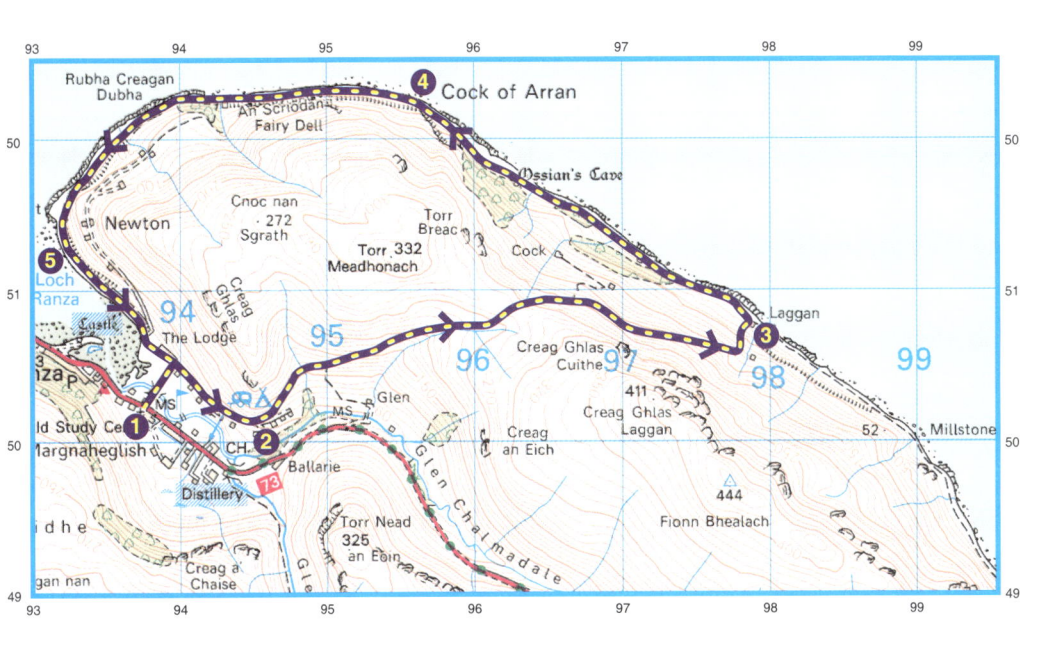

Sunrise on a Snowy Arran

Walk 25: Clauchland Hills, Arran

Grade: B Distance: 8 miles, THC 250 metres Tracks & minor road

Choose a sunny day to enjoy Arran at its best and take the walk at a leisurely pace to enjoy the views. The walk starts at Brodick Pier. Suggest taking the 0945am ferry from Ardrossan to arrive at Brodick pier where the walk starts. (NS021360)

1 From the pier turn left up Lamlash Road. At the signpost to Corrygills, 2nd left, turn left. Follow this road as far as it goes. The tarred road becomes a cart track. (NS042342) Turn left at sign for Dun Fionn.

2 Look for a signpost on the right pointing to a path to Lamlash. Go up the path to Dun Fionn to the trig point in the centre of the old fort. (NS046338)

3 From here turn west along the ridge, enjoying the fine views on both sides of Brodick Bay, Lamlash Bay, Holy island and the towering Goatfell. The path drops down to forest track. Turn right to the Brodick-Lamlash Road. (NS018333)

4 Cross the road and enter the forest following a sign to Glen Cloy. From here it is downhill most of the way. Continue on the forest path and eventually the path turns east towards Brodick. (NR993341)

5 Cross the burn and make your way across a field, keeping to the track all the way. The track emerges opposite the Golf Course. (NS011360)

6 Turn right along the road which will bring you back to Brodick pier in time to catch the ferry at 1645pm.

Brodick Pier

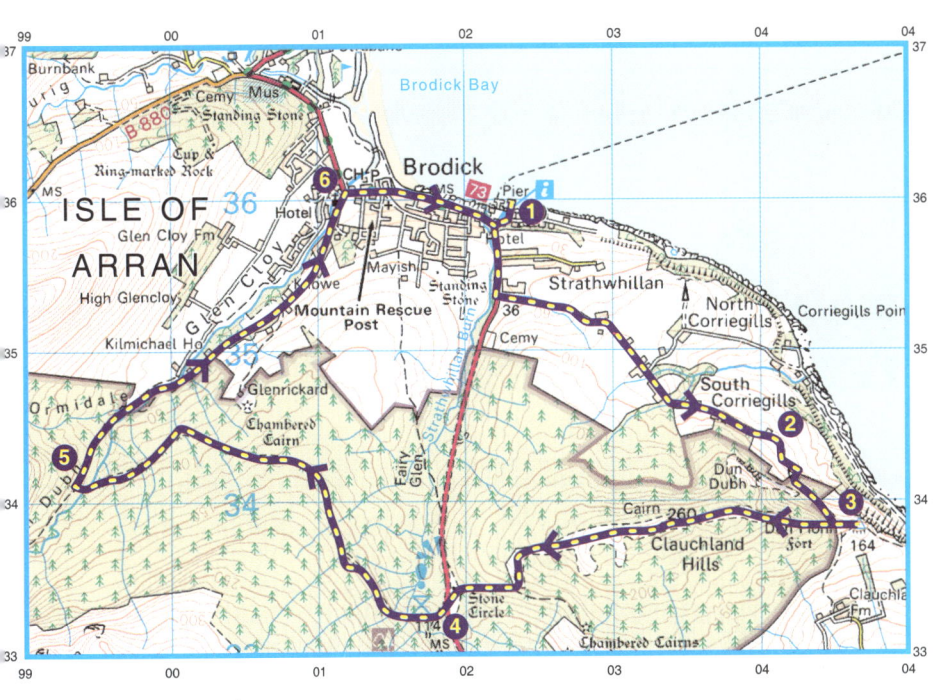

Nearly there!

53

Photograph Gallery

The Calm Before The Storm!

Autumn Colours

Burns Statue, Irvine

Portencross Castle

View From Irish Law

Forest Walk, Dalry

Holy Isle from Clauchland Hills

Tarryholme Pond Residents' Association!

Ramblers Anonymous!

Enjoy a good walk ...
... in good company

Meet new friends, get fit and stay healthy. Walking is the best form of exercise, to enjoy anytime, anyplace with anyone. From a stroll down your local path to a scramble up a mountain ridge, there is a route for you.

Join today and get 20% off.

A year's membership will give you:

- membership of a local walking group providing an unrivalled choice of walks every week of the year;
- the award winning quarterly magazine walk;
- a twice yearly Newsletter to keep you up to date with issues in Scotland;
- Walk Britain guide packed with useful information about places to walk and stay; and
- discretionary discounts in many outdoor stores.

Join us today! You are sure of a great welcome!

Visit www.ramblers.org.uk/offer or call us on 020 7339 8595 quoting code CL9.

For enquiries about our walking groups email us at Scotland@ramblers.org.uk or telephone 01577 861222.

Offer is not available to existing members.

The Ramblers Scotland

www.ramblers.org.uk

The Ramblers' Association is a Registered Charity, England & Wales no. 1093577, Scotland no. SC039799

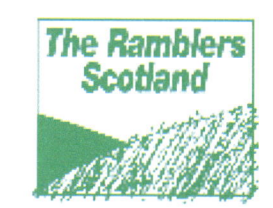